MW01295145

FOCUSING-ORIENTED THERAPY

FOCUSING-ORIENTED THERAPY

(FOT)

A Contribution to the Practice, Teaching,
And Understanding of Focusing-Oriented
Psychotherapy

Neil Friedman, Ph.D.

iUniverse, Inc.
New York Lincoln Shanghai

Focusing-Oriented Therapy
(Fot)

Copyright © 2007 by Neil Friedman

All rights reserved. No part of this book may be used or reproduced by any means, graphic, electronic, or mechanical, including photocopying, recording, taping or by any information storage retrieval system without the written permission of the publisher except in the case of brief quotations embodied in critical articles and reviews.

iUniverse books may be ordered through booksellers or by contacting:

iUniverse
2021 Pine Lake Road, Suite 100
Lincoln, NE 68512
www.iuniverse.com
1-800-Authors (1-800-288-4677)

cover photo © Abraham Menashe

ISBN-13: 978-0-595-39830-0 (pbk)
ISBN-13: 978-0-595-84234-6 (ebk)
ISBN-10: 0-595-39830-8 (pbk)
ISBN-10: 0-595-84234-8 (ebk)

Printed in the United States of America

For

Gene

Responses point.
—Eugene Gendlin

In most books the I…is omitted; in this it will be retained…it is, after all, always the first person who is speaking…Moreover, I…require of every writer…a simple and sincere account of his own life, and not merely what he has heard of other…lives.
—Henry David Thoreau

The conclusion is inescapable: to become a better therapist one must become a better (more loving) person.
—Andras Angyal

Contents

Introduction

For thirty years, except for vacations and occasional illnesses, I have been doing ten to fifteen hours of psychotherapy a week. Seventy per cent of that time has been individual therapy. Thirty per cent has been couples therapy. I have also, with my co-leader, Dr. Joan Klagsbrun, trained about one hundred students to do therapy.

My work has been guided by the approach of Dr. Eugene Gendlin. He was the first supervisor of my therapy and my second therapist. When I first met him, he called his work Experiential Psychotherapy. He had described it in a series of important papers (Gendlin, e.g., 1961, 1967, 1968).

Sometime later Gendlin changed the name of his therapy to Focusing-Oriented Psychotherapy and published a text by that name (1996).

I consider that book and the previously cited articles to be the bases for Focusing-Oriented Therapy. I am happy to associate my work with that orientation, so long as I can also indicate my points of divergence from Gendlin's model. [1]

♦

I am not entirely happy with Gendlin's name for this new brand of therapy. I am inclined to refer to it intermittently as Focusing-Oriented, Felt Sense-Oriented, or simply Gendlinian therapy. It is a therapy originated by Eugene Gendlin, built around his concept of the felt sense, and making use of focusing as one major intervention. It is his distinctively different approach to therapy. It has a deep philosophical background to it. As I will show, calling it Focusing-Oriented-Therapy does not really do it justice. But, given that that is now the accepted term, I will use it most frequently in this book.

Gendlin's words point to the difficulty with calling his approach Focusing-Oriented Therapy. He writes that in therapy, "the relationship (of therapist and client)...is of first importance, listening second, and focusing instructions come only third" (p.297). If they come only third, why name the therapy after them?

There is another issue. As we shall see, focusing is a *method*, a *technique* that Gendlin discovered and developed. In the minds of many he is inextricably intertwined with it and it with him. To name his therapy after this method is to suggest that it is a technique-oriented therapy. It is not. It is not just an application of the focusing method to therapy. It is so much more than that.

◆

Terminological issues aside, in this book I want to make a contribution to the practice, teaching, and understanding of Focusing-Oriented Therapy.

Part One provides the **key** terms necessary to understand FOT, an account of my own therapy with Gendlin that helps show how he practices FOT, and a chapter on the therapeutic relationship, which is central to FOT.

Part Two takes up each of the key **methods** in FOT—focusing and listening—and illustrates ways to combine them in therapy.

Part Three makes a distinction between what I call **verbal** and **body-centered** therapies and illustrates how focusing and listening can be combined with certain verbal exchanges and body-centered methods.

The Appendices provide what I call a roadmap through Gendlin's book, Focusing-Oriented Psychotherapy, and my own version of focusing instructions. Gendlin's is a brilliant and dense book. I try to make it more accessible.

My own commentary on FOT may be found scattered throughout the book. How I differ from Gendlin's point of view is particularly emphasized in Chapters Two and Seven.

◆

FOT is a relative newcomer on the therapeutic scene. It has a lot to offer to therapy to help make it more therapeutic. How therapeutic is therapy? Certainly more so than Eysenck, (1961) once wrote but less so than its current acolytes affirm. Psychotherapy is a mixed bag. It is important to remember that people mostly go into therapy out of personal misery. Going to a therapist is a bet one makes on improving one's life. It ought not be like going to OTB (off-track betting).

A colleague has had ten different individual therapists for some duration during his twenty-three years of being in therapy. Five of them have been excellent. His experiences with them have been very helpful. That is the good news. Here is the bad news. Five of them have been of no help or minimal help. That is fifty percent. I am not even counting another ten that he has had just for one session and not continued with. Nor have I mentioned yet his eight couples' therapists, six of whom did not do much good.

It is difficult to feel sanguine about these numbers. Especially if you are the one who is doing the living during these hit-and-miss experiences of supposed helpfulness.

Therapy and the individual therapist gone to may be one of the most important choices one makes in one's life. It is incumbent upon therapists and writers about therapy that we do whatever we can to make therapy a more positive experience than it sometimes is. I hope that my contribution helps carry focusing-oriented therapy (FOT) forward and, through it, all of the therapy world. My aim is no less than that. The need is no less than that.

Part One:

Bases of Focusing-Oriented Therapy

One

Key Terms in Focusing-Oriented Psychotherapy

Eugene Gendlin is a philosopher who was pulled into psychology by the question: How does raw experience get symbolized? Beginning with this question he has gone on to develop his own approach to psychotherapy.

Gendlin's key term is *experiencing*. Persons are experiencing processes. We apprehend the world moment-to-moment through our experiencing of it. A flow of experiencing is always ongoing in a living human being.

Gendlin uses the term experiencing "to denote concrete experience…the raw, present, ongoing {flow} of what is usually called experience." The term refers to "the flow of feeling, concretely, to which you can at every moment attend inwardly, if you wish." He continues:

> It is something so simple, so easily available to every person that at first its very simplicity makes it hard to point to. Another term for it is felt meaning or feeling. However, feeling is a word usually used for (specific feelings)…But regardless of the many changes in what we feel—that is to say, really, how we feel—there always is the concretely present flow of feeling (Gendlin 1997, 3, 6).

What is particularly "human" about human nature is experiencing. Gendlin provides an example:

> First, feel your body. Your body can, of course, be looked at from the outside. But I am asking you to feel it from the inside. There you are. There, as simply put as possible, is your experiencing of the moment, now.

He concludes of experiencing, "Notice. It is always there for you"(Gendlin 1997, 7, 13).

With his well-known emphasis on the "here and now" Fritz Perls was the cheerleader for experiencing. Gendlin is its philosopher. Experiencing is our primary way of comprehending an ever changing now. What does this imply? Before we have explicit words, concepts, or other symbols, we understand the now viscerally through our experiencing of it. Cognition does not come first. Perception does not come first. Language does not come first. Experiencing comes first. Human beings are not bundles of complexes, traits, or other contents. Human beings are not their thinking process. Human beings are their experiencing process.

What are the characteristics of experiencing?

Experiencing is *bodily felt*, "rather than thought, known or verbalized." It is concrete lived experience rather than constructs, abstractions. or generalizations about experience. It is *pre-conceptual*. It is there before concepts. It is *internally differentiable*—that is, different concepts can be made from it and thus different vocabularies can be used to speak of the same bit of experiencing. This is because it has *implicit richness*. There is always a "more" in any experiencing than can be made explicit at any moment. That is why Gendlin calls his overall work The Philosophy of the Implicit. Finally, experiencing can be the object of *direct reference*. One can at any moment turn one's attention inside and "tune into", "look at", or "listen to" one's experiencing (Gendlin 1961, 234).

♦

When I make direct reference to my experiencing, Gendlin calls what I find a *felt sense*, a term that he coined. A felt sense is a "bodily felt, implicitly rich sense of some situation, problem, or aspect of one's life" It is "the holistic, implicit, bodily sense of a complex situation" (Gendlin 1996, 20, 58).

How is one to be towards the felt sense, towards the bodily felt experiencing? It is important to take *the focusing attitude* towards one's own experiencing. This attitude can be described as anything from an acknowledging to a welcoming to a being friendly to or to an embracing of the felt sense. The felt sense needs to be treated nice.

Human beings can have a felt sense of almost anything. *This is most important to understand.* Stop for a moment. Go inward. Take a moment between questions: What is your felt sense of right now? What is your felt sense of yourself? What is your felt sense of your health? What is your felt sense of your career? What is your felt sense of your relationship situation? What is your felt sense of the world situation? What is your felt sense of me?

For Gendlin, the felt sense is crucial to psychotherapy. Psychotherapy begins to be therapeutic when one makes direct reference to one's felt sense of the problem, issue, or situation upon which one is working. By staying with the felt sense and finding a symbol that matches it, the felt sense unfolds its meanings and shifts. This *felt shift*—another term Gendlin coined—is the feeling of therapeutic change actually happening. Psychotherapy, from this point of view, is a series of steps of finding felt senses, being friendly to them, accurately symbolizing them, and then feeling felt shifts.

Here is a simple example of a felt sense and how to begin to process it. What is my feeling of my writing right now? What is my felt sense of it? My felt sense is in my belly. The handle for it is "turgid…struggling…trying too hard to make my point." When I thus symbolize the felt sense, I feel more relaxed and calm. I go back to my writing from the now more relaxed place.

The felt sense can also be a present experiencing of a past event. What is my felt sense now of how I felt this morning when my computer froze? The felt sense is in the scrunching of my face, and the words are "irritated...frustrated...stymied." When I say, "stymied", which feels most accurate, my face relaxes, and I feel better.

The felt sense can also be my present experiencing of a long-ago event, such as a trauma. How do I feel now about the eye operation that I had when I was four years old? The feeling is in my chest, and the words are "sad...sorrowful...about how much it affected me...especially the being left "(in the hospital). After I say "especially the being left", there is a tear and a shift inside. I feel relief.

◆

Let me return now to the language of experiencing and say some of this over. The following words are most important for therapists, clients, and therapists in training: For therapy to succeed it must make contact with the client's experiencing process. There has to be a felt dimension to therapy. "Genuine psychotherapy {begins} at the point of going beyond the intellectual approach by helping the patient to an immediate, present experiencing of his problems."(1961, 234). The therapist aims to give what Gendlin calls *the experiential response:* that is, a response that points at the experiencing process in the client. The best therapeutic response is one that has "a concrete experiential effect in the {client}" (Gendlin 1968, 208).

In one of his best essays, "The Experiential Response", (1968), Gendlin shows that when they succeed, both a client-centered reflection of feeling response and a psychoanalytic interpretation work in the same way. One has to bring in the concept of experiencing to draw out this important similarity.

Gendlin says that "a good client-centered response formulates the felt, implicit meaning of the client's present experiencing." Similarly, "an effective interpretation must somehow help the patient deal with the inner experiencing to which the interpretation refers...to grapple with it, face it, tolerate it, and work it through."

Drawing on his theory of experiencing and the experiential response, Gendlin formulates a hypothesis about therapeutic outcomes: "The greater the role played by experiencing during the therapy hours, the greater will be the therapeutic change and {the more likely} the successful outcome of therapy" (Gendlin 1961, 240, 243).

To test this hypothesis, Gendlin and his colleagues developed and tested The Experiencing Scale, which measures the level of experiencing in a segment of therapy. To date, more than thirty studies show that a higher experiencing level correlates with more successful therapy (Hendricks 2002).

♦

Experiencing, the experiential response, the experiencing scale, the focusing attitude, the felt sense, the felt shift—these are terms I will return to over and over in the pages ahead. They are crucial to an understanding of felt-sense oriented therapy.

We need to take one further step to grasp another of Gendlin's many contributions to the psychotherapy field. That is the step to specific methods and their combination.

As we have seen, Gendlin formulated what he says a response must do in order to be therapeutic. It must make contact with the client's ongoing, bodily felt, experiencing process. Next, Gendlin asked whether this skill could be taught. If we know what people have to do to make progress in therapy, can we teach people how to do that thing? Gendlin calls this skill *focusing*. Focusing is a precise specification of what successful clients do in therapy. It is what makes therapy work. For forty years, Gendlin has been teaching people how to focus. This is what he is best known for in psychological circles. Focusing can be used in therapy. The therapist can teach the client to focus, sometimes through small steps of instruction giving. Focusing is a therapeutic intervention that flows out of Gendlin's perspective on psychotherapy.

Listening is another. Listening is focusing's fraternal twin. It is not as original to Gendlin as focusing is. Experiential listening is Carl Rogers' "reflection of feelings" response reconceptualized in the light of the experiencing concept.

In Gendlin's therapy, focusing and listening are the basic therapeutic skills. They provide two ways to make contact with the client's experiencing process and help it move forward. They are not the only ways to do so. Gendlin's book, Focusing-Oriented Psychotherapy is not just about focusing and listening. It also includes chapters on role-playing, imagery, dream work, cognitive methods, action steps, working with the critic, other bodily methods and catharsis. Gendlin shows how all these methods can be used so as to make contact with a felt sense and produce a felt shift.

Keeping in his or her awareness the concepts of the felt sense and the felt shift, the Gendlinian therapist knows how to combine whatever other methods he or she practices, not as an eclectic hodge-podge, but in a manner that is guided by a systematic framework that includes a theory of human nature and the nature of personality change.

Gendlin's is a powerful framework. I hope and trust that it will be better known and appreciated in the years ahead.

Now, let us see how I was introduced to this approach.

Two

Eugene Gendlin's Practice and Theory of Focusing-Oriented Therapy

As I have said, in several papers and a book, Eugene Gendlin has put forth his own systematic approach to psychotherapy. It comes out of phenomenological philosophy and Rogerian psychotherapy (Gendlin 1974; Hart 1970). It provides an alternative to, say, an analytic, cognitive-behavioral, gestalt, or psychopharmacological approach to therapy. Just as there are Freudian, Jungian, Adlerian, and Reichian approaches to therapy, there is a Gendlinian approach. It is systematic. It has its own vocabulary, its own philosophical stance, its own kind of concepts[1], its own linkage of concepts, its own methods, and its own way of combining methods. It is a very distinctive though not all that well-known approach.

In the first chapter I have introduced the basic terms needed to grasp Gendlin's point of view. I see the experiencing process, the felt sense, the felt shift, the experiencing scale, the focusing attitude, experiential focusing and experiential listening as fundamental terms for understanding his approach.

Gendlin is not just a theorist. He is also a therapist (although, as he likes to remind audiences, his only higher degree is a Ph.D. in philosophy) I will move on now to talk about Gendlin as a therapist.

♦

Gendlin was my second therapist. I saw him for over a year starting in 1976 after I had seen an existential psychiatrist, Leida Berg, M.D. for three years (Friedman 2005). I went to see him again in 1994. From my two experiences with him, what can I say about him as a therapist?

First—and most importantly—*his practice very much follows his theory*. I would estimate that upwards of seventy-five percent of my therapy time with Gendlin consisted of focusing and listening.

Here are some excerpts from an unexceptional session in 1974. It is the only session with him that I ever taped. I don't recall why I taped this particular session. Notice the particular way that Gendlin listens. It is subtler than simply "saying back". He uses language very carefully to help evoke the experiential response.

I had just gotten my first consulting job. Gendlin helps me sort out my feelings about it:

NF: Right now, I feel so good that it's hard to…They really like me and I'm not sure what I feel…There's something in my feelings…It feels delightful how much they want me…I guess I'm not sure I trust it, but more than that I've lost a sense of what *I* feel…I mean—

EG: So it's *wonderful* how much they want you but *somewhere* in there you've lost touch with what *you* feel.

NF: I mean, I'm sending all the right signals but I'm in touch with something about being afraid…

EG: *Someplace* you're scared.

I am already speaking at a high experiencing level. Gendlin's listening responses introduce the 'place' idea. "Somewhere…someplace" there is further feeling.

NF: Yeah…my feelings sometimes feel…so superficial…

EG: (picking up on my non-verbal behavior) There's something that doesn't even want to consider that…that it's silly or something…but if you let it be the way it is, then there's something (in a tentative tone) thin or wrong or superficial or something in your feelings?

Gendlin's use of the 'something' in his response leaves it an open question what actually is there. Now, after some careful listening, he adds a focusing invitation onto this open-ended listening response:

EG: Can you touch that feeling?
NF: (eyes closed, pause) Confused. I am really confused.

Focusing has started to clarify the feeling.

EG: Yeah, stay there…

His intention is to keep me focusing.

NF: I'm afraid their feelings about me will change…That feels heavy.
EG: So, there's some feeling there…some heavy certainty…that their feeling about you won't last.

His listening response is right on target.

NF: Yes! I want it too much…
EG: Anything I want *that badly*…
NF: No. Not anything. Just *this* kind of thing.
EG: Oh! (Genuine surprise) It is just *this* that won't work. Some sureness there…what is that sureness?
NF: (Pause. Eyes closed. Going inside.) I can't sustain this level of working for too long. I'm too inconsistent and cyclic. My own fear will get in the way.

There is a lot here and Gendlin feeds it back to me one thing at a time.

EG: So there's a fear thing…
NF: Yeah.

EG: A cyclic thing…

NF: Yeah.

EG: Oh, and also an inconsistent thing.

NF: Yeah…all three…together.

EG: (focusing invitation) Go see what all that is…

NF: (focusing) Fear.

EG: It's fear.

NF: (slightly louder) Fear…of the not lasting.

EG: Ah…The fear is of the not lasting.

NF: (In response to this 'experiential response') Wait! Something just happened. This is remarkable…It just changed…I *can* do it! I *really* can.

EG: Now…slowly here…there's a Big Shift there…

NF: Yeah.

EG: You went from fearful to real solid and confident there.

NF: Yeah. Suddenly, I feel real clear.

EG: You are in a different place.

Again, the 'place' notion.

NF: Yes…not entirely new. I went from the fear to the confidence…that is not so unusual for me…They are each so *total*…

EG: Yeah…That is what is so…(searching for the word)…*surprising* there. You gain the one and lose the other. And it goes both ways?

He is asking out of genuine curiosity.

NF: Exactly!

EG: You almost forget the other side.

NF: No! Not 'almost'…Entirely.

EG: Entirely!

NF: They are two entirely different body states…Ah, it's Angyal! It is Andras Angyal's two systems (Angyal 1965). It is the pattern of neurosis and the pattern of health. I have written about them theoretically before. I'm feeling them…their oscillation…

EG: Hey! Let's mark that. (He writes 'fear' and 'confidence' in pencil on the wall above me.) You've actually been feeling those two total orientations.

NF: Yes! (Tape ends here)

Notice that in this session I get to *experience* and have named a shift in orientations for which I already have a theoretical vocabulary. Gendlin is mostly doing listening and focusing with me. He keeps suggesting that there is a 'something' inside. This is done quite subtly. It is in his choice of words. I was not consciously aware of it until just now when I transcribed the tape. I experience a Big Shift and leave the session thinking much more clearly and feeling much better than when I came in.

I experienced him as really being with me, really following my lead here. In terms of attachment theory, Gendlin's exquisite and highly sensitive listening and focusing help this session (and the whole therapy) become "a secure base' where I feel quite distinctly seen and heard on a moment-to-moment basis (Holmes 2001).

◆

Gendlin did not do only focusing and listening with me. This is important. Three other specific interventions stand out in my memory of my therapy with him. The first two come from our sessions in the seventies.

For one session, at my initiative, we took the elevator down from his apartment and sat outdoors on a bench facing the East River. It was the anniversary of my father's death. I had Gendlin put his arm around me as I related to him as an ideal father and then remove it as I related to him as my real father. He accommodated *(Pesso 1988)* by role-playing both parts as I took turns experiencing and talking to each.

At times I would step out of the role-play and talk to him as himself, my therapist. Gendlin would then say, "Uh-huh," and give a brief listening response to what I had said. Off and on in the session, I cried.

There were many felt senses and felt shifts. As I write this now, I remember how close we sat and the feel of his arm around me and even now, my eyes tear up.

I have written about the next session previously, camouflaging it by making myself the therapist with a nameless client (Friedman 1982). In the session, I was experiencing my self-criticism. I was talking about how diminished I was feeling, how "hapless, helpless, and hopeless." This is how I was feeling about myself. Gendlin told me *not* to focus there. He said, "This is a place where focusing doesn't work." He explained that there was at that moment a powerful "criticizer" part of me and a powerless "criticized" part of me. We had been over this ground in an exploratory way several times before. Gendlin instructed me how to "reverse roles"; that is, how to become the powerful criticizer part while he sat in for the powerless criticized part. He instructed me *to do to him what I was doing to myself*—and to do it both verbally and non-verbally. He suggested that I get up, stand over him, really get into it...and not physically hurt him. In gestalt, this method is called 'undoing retroflection' (Naranjo n.d.).

I stood over him shouting critical statements ("You are worthless," "You will never amount to anything") and jabbing with my index finger in his direction. My finger got quite close to his face. He cowered in the chair fearfully. At a certain point he instructed me to drop the words and just exaggerate the non-verbal activity.

It happened that this session was taking place in his son's bedroom. I spied a rubber pirate's knife on a shelf on the wall. Spontaneously, I grabbed the knife and started stabbing the air right in front of Gendlin's face. I stabbed at him several times and then suddenly had an image (not a memory) of my father standing over me stabbing me with his criticisms. I burst into tears and fell into a chair. I cried a lot and really got where that 'critic' part of me came from. The session was very cathartic, and I remember it as having had a very significant impact on my self-critical tendencies.

My third memory comes from twenty years later. In October 1994, I was living in Arlington, Mass. Gendlin was in Wellesley, Mass. while his daughter attended a school in the Boston area.

I remember starting one of our early sessions by saying, "I feel as if I have ruined my life." Gendlin responded that he had this principle that a person had the right to ruin his life as many times as he needed to.

His response surprised me. He had heard the self-accusation ("You fool! Look what you have done!") that I did not know was embedded in my sentence. He had responded to that which I did not even recognize was in me at the time. His words went right through me. He had silenced the critic. In response, first I smiled and then I began to sob.

I cried for several minutes. Then, my mind was quite suddenly clear. During the rest of the session I teased out four distinct strands of grief that I was carrying around. One was for my father's death— twenty-six years previous. One was for the death of my marriage. I do not remember what the other strands were for. For each strand of grief I cried the tears that felt connected to that strand. They were different sums and kinds of tears. The session was extremely **cathartic** and extremely clarifying. My journal indicates that I felt much better for about three months after this session.

I cite these three sessions for a few reasons. First, they suggest how much of my therapy with Gendlin centered on my father and my own self-critical tendencies. These subjects were not taken care of in my therapy with Leida Berg. They were major in my therapy with Gendlin. I did not cover everything in any single therapy I have had. A 'layering' of therapy has been important to me so that in different therapies I have dealt primarily with different troubling aspects of my life (McKenna and Todd 1997). There has also been considerable overlap and with aging the appearance of yet new problems and challenges.

Second, these sessions illustrate how Gendlin did more than just focusing and listening with me. Notice that there is even one instance where he warns me *against* focusing. This is very important. It happened a few times in my work with him. It indicates that his Focusing-Oriented

Therapy is *not* an exclusively Focusing Therapy. That is one common misconception about his work that I want to clear up in this book.

And, third, these sessions suggest how much Gendlin uses the interaction between therapist and client. Please remember that, as we saw in the introduction, he puts the interaction of therapist and client as the primary avenue affecting all the other work going on in the therapy. The literal breath of fresh air in the first example and his physical touch were important to its outcome. In the second example he does not act like the stereotyped Rogerian therapist. He is functioning more in a gestalt mode. And in the third example one could say that Gendlin has deftly interpreted what was not conscious to me as being in my words and thus has helped carry my experiencing forward from where it had been badly stuck for some time.

Here is a further word about work with the critic. In the focusing tradition I see two different ways to work with the critic (Gendlin 1996; Weiser-Cornell 2005). The latter comes from a perspective that Weiser-Cornell calls "the radical acceptance of everything" (2005). Her emphasis is on the positive role the critic is trying to serve. She says the other way does not work. When she says this so sweepingly, she is wrong. My own experience contradicts her generalization. Gendlin is more likely to wave off the critic or tell it to go take a hike. He quite specifically argues against giving it a Rogerian style 'neutral' listening.

I have only experienced Gendlin's approach to the critic and have found it exceedingly helpful.

◆

Gendlin makes mistakes. In fact, he builds making mistakes into his conception of therapy. He writes that:

> A therapist does not need the appearance of always being right. Indeed, that appearance should be avoided. It is an unreasonable and unfair demand some therapists put on themselves...Early in therapy, whenever I have said something that turns out to be wrong, I point out my mistake

explicitly. I need the client to see that I do not have trouble being wrong…Once clients know this, it is easy for them to correct me, and tell me what does come inside them when it is not what I thought…(1996, 105).

One of Gendlin's most well chosen metaphors has to do with what the therapist ought to do when he finds he has made a mistake:

> The way to respond is simple. It is something like discovering that you are standing on someone's toes. You do not argue, you just move your foot off the person's toes. But you do not go home, or sit down and cry, or apologize overly profusely as if what you did is more than you can stand. You just say you did not intend to stand on their toes, and then you do not go right back to standing on their toes again. It is the difference between the other person's rightful space, and your own. You keep your space, and you instantly get out of theirs (1996, 110).

In context, these remarks refer to mistakes in what the therapist says within a session. But there are other kinds of mistakes too. In fact, Gendlin made the same mistake in both my times with him, twenty years apart.

I want to make clear that what follows is not offered in any spirit of 'Gendlin-bashing.' He is a fallible human being, not a god. He does not want to be treated like a god. I do not think of him as one. It does him or his theory no favor to omit any aspect of the real live human events that went on in my therapy with him. In fact, when I read cases and see a therapist can be and admit that he is wrong, I feel more trusting of his other reports of success. With me Gendlin made mistakes that go beyond even his fine words about mistakes.

Both times he gave me just one session's notice that the therapy had to end because he was leaving town.

Please note that what I might now call 'sudden unforeseen abandonment' was central to my troubles in life (Friedman 2005). It boggles my mind that I lived through this twice with Gendlin.

In the seventies, he did not get the teaching job in New York that he had expected so as to extend his three-year stay. He did not know for sure that he was leaving until just before he told me. But he had not prepared me for this eventuality.

I responded like a good soldier. It happened that on the morning of our last session, *The New York Times* had on its front page the picture of a swarthy-looking tennis coach who would no longer be teaching his long-time pupil. (Tiriac and Nastase) I latched onto the story. I was the accomplished tennis player saying good-bye to his coach. I congratulated both of us on how successful our work together had been. I celebrated my readiness to move on. Gendlin and I shared a fulsome hug and a good-feeling good-bye.

He left town. I got depressed.

The second time, in 1994, Gendlin gave me the impression that he would be in town for a couple of years while his daughter attended a school for talented kids. I had no reason to doubt this. I needed the therapy badly. I was in worse shape than when I had seen him in New York. And the therapy was being quite helpful.

I was out of town and missed a session at the end of August 1994. Two days later I was talking on the phone with a mutual friend. She told me that Gendlin wanted me to call him so that he could tell me that our next session would be our last as his daughter had decided not to return to the school and so the family would be leaving town.

I don't have words to adequately describe how I immediately felt. I was silent. I was thoroughly shocked. I said, aloud "Unbelievable". I saw the repeated pattern in his sudden unforeseen leaving and the significance of that pattern in my life. I could not believe it was all happening again.

I was furious. I phoned him and got the message from him. I kept the call brief. After, I started shaking my head from side to side in disbelief and stomping around the room.

The next Tuesday I came into our last session very, very mad. I lectured Gendlin on his therapeutic irresponsibility. He listened and reflected my feelings back until I told him that I didn't want to hear my words from him. I said some awful things about him. I threw in every criticism of him that I had ever felt and a few that I had merely heard second hand. I loved him and I was unmerciful to him. He was penitent. I would not let him off the hook. I told him that his abrupt leaving even undid some of the good work we had done together. That bothered him. I wanted to bother him. I shared with him my utter amazement that I was living through a second sudden abandonment with him. I related it to my larger abandonment issue. "How could you…" was my sentiment.

When the hour was over I would not look at him and I would not say good-bye. I would not agree to keep in touch with him. I let him know that I would do nothing to help him assuage his guilt. As I walked down the stairs from his second floor apartment, I heard knocking on the wall above me. My back was to him. I smiled as I remembered—in the midst of my fury—his article about his work with schizophrenics and the ingenious ways he would communicate his feelings to them without using words (1967).

He was saying good-bye.

I fumed for a good while. Days passed. Our mutual friend told me he had telephoned her and said he was worried about me and that I should call him to let him know that I was okay. I didn't call until I damn well felt like it.

I was down that he was gone, but I did not fall into a deeper depression. Leaving with my anger expressed helped me more than leaving in peace had twenty years before. By this time I had had other therapeutic experiences with full expression of my anger (Friedman 1982). I believe that anger will never be easy for me. But, this time I had done my anger justice and, to use a theoretical construct from Angyal, my 'healthy system' was happy. My reaction to Gendlin's second leaving was a sign of progress.

These two examples illustrate the fact that therapists have lives and families and that endings of therapy are not always in the hands of clients. I believe that therapists have an obligation to prepare clients for endings as best they can. We cannot banish the unforeseen ending of therapy completely from our reality. But if, as Rilke puts it, "So we live, forever taking leave," we therapists can do our best to keep unannounced leave-takings to an absolute minimum (Rilke 1994).

I stayed mad at Gendlin for awhile. Eventually we reconciled and resumed our friendship and colleagueship. He said that our connection was "thick." He is right. That is one reason why I can write this chapter and this book as I have.

◆

In conclusion, what did I get from my therapy with Gendlin? And what do I have to say about his theoretical framework?

◆

In this section I will take up the first question. In the final section I will take up the second.

Most of all, from our work I got much of my professional identity. Gendlin teaches focusing. I teach focusing. Gendlin features listening. I feature listening. Gendlin is a focusing oriented psychotherapist. I am a focusing oriented psychotherapist.

There are differences. I am not a Gene Gendlin clone. But, I have presented over one hundred focusing workshops at professional conferences. I have contributed fifteen articles to *The Focusing Connection*. I have published four books with the word Focusing in the title. I am an integral and valued part of the focusing network. When I am known in psychological circles, it is most often for my work with focusing.

This suggests that professional role modeling is one thing that the successful psychotherapist does for a psychotherapist-client in treatment. I learned how to be a therapist—and how to be as a therapist—primarily by being in successive therapies that acquainted me first-hand with various methods, theories, styles, and ways of being. For me these were more valuable experiences professionally than my graduate training had been. Gendlin's has been the most valuable.

Beyond the professional, looking back on my therapy experiences in the seventies, I did not change as much from my therapy with Gendlin as I did from my therapy with Leida Berg. In 1978 I wrote in my journal, "Gene provided the fine tuning. Leida turned on the switch."

She opened me to my feeling life. My therapy with her led to my being much more present to my here and now experiencing. My 'experiencing level' rose dramatically. And there were profound life-changes too. My digestion cleared up. I gained weight. I became a psychotherapist. I got to know my anger. The "me" whom I knew at the end of therapy with her was significantly different from the 'me' whom I had known when I started therapy with her.

My work with Gendlin *built upon* my work with Leida. There was an unplanned synergy. Gendlin provided focusing and listening which gave me a finer discernment of my affective life. He provided concepts and language that helped me hold onto and better describe the affective changes I was experiencing in myself. He helped me become less self-critical. He contributed remarkably to my confidence in myself as a therapist. The subtle nuances of felt senses were added to the dramatic experience of emotionality that happened with Leida. This particular 'layering' of therapeutic experiences was quite fortunate.

I do not know what would have been the process or outcome if the order in which I saw them had been reversed. I am happy that I saw them in the order I did.

In 1994 Gendlin's help was invaluable as I struggled with a long, deep, major depression. We did not beat it. But we gave it a good run for its money. To use the pugilistic image of an analyst, Allen Wheelis (2005) in 1994 Gendlin and I fought my demons to a draw.

What do I have to say about Gendlin's theoretical framework? Throughout this book I will comment upon it several times. For now what I want to say is that *sometimes* Gendlin writes as if *all* therapeutic change can be reduced to *his* theory of therapeutic change. He makes sweeping claims for his way of doing therapy. When he does so, he goes too far. When he doesn't—when he recognizes his own way of conceiving and doing therapy as another real good way and one that can be combined with whatever else the therapist already knows and does—then he makes a very significant contribution to the literature of theoretical frameworks of therapy.

This distinction is quite important. I sometimes think of it as the conquistador vs. the collaborator stance of the focusing-oriented therapist. Consider this statement from Focusing-Oriented Psychotherapy. I think it is one of Gendlin's better statements about the relation of his work to that of others:

> The therapist should keep in mind that focusing is one way to carry implicit bodily experiencing forward, but there are other ways. Other ways of working (for example) through interaction, imagery, dreams, changes in habit and in action—though they are made more effective by focusing, can also constitute therapy without it. No one has the right to claim that there is only one way for human beings to grow, in therapy, in personal development, or in anything (1996, 108).

Gendlin needs to keep this sentence in mind and be consistent with it throughout his writings.

People can change in psychotherapy without focusing. Gendlin does not always allow for this possibility. For example, he writes, "a therapeutic response always aims at the client's own directly felt sense of what he is talking about"(1968, 213). The culprit here is that 'always.' In the same paper, he writes as his eighth rule of therapy that "only referent movement [i.e. change in the experiencing process] is progress" (1968, 216). Not so. Anything that helps a client is progress. Anything that helps a client is therapeutic.

The problem is not just in this particular paper. In his groundbreaking book *Experiencing and the Creation of Meaning* (1961/1997) Gendlin writes, "without experiencing we have no theoretical account of therapeutic personality change, or even its possibility"(p.39). Again, in the same book, he writes, "there is in all therapy a working with inner experiencing." (p.52). And again, "Section A of this chapter will make two assertions: (a) experiencing plays a vital role in therapeutic change; (b) terms that refer to experiencing are required in the theory of psychotherapy" (1997, 227).

These are overstatements. When Gendlin says in the same article that the best therapeutic response is one that has a concrete experiential effect in the individual I have to say again—not so. The best therapeutic response is one that is helpful, regardless of whether it conforms to one or another of psychotherapeutic theories.

Consider three clients of my own.

Client A has a Ph.D. in Geography, works in a bank, and wants to become an opera singer. He came to me after another focusing-oriented therapist took a sabbatical. My client had not been able to learn how to focus. I tried for a while to help him focus. He could not link his feelings to what they were about. We both experienced a lot of feelings of failure as I tried unsuccessfully to teach him focusing. After a while, I stopped trying to teach him to focus. Instead, we talked. We talked about the changes he wanted to make in his life. I made suggestions and reinforced all his efforts in the direction of change in profession. We joked about his inability to focus and my inability to teach him focusing. His depression and anxiety diminished some, and he made progress in the direction in which he wanted to go. He never got focusing but he did make progress as our relationship developed.

Client B: He is in computer work. As a child his mother would ask him what he was feeling and then contradict whatever he said. This was a constant source of humiliation to him. He was allergic to focusing. We made no progress by my asking him what he was feeling. Mostly we talked about what was going on in his life and what changes he wanted to make. These were both job-related and relationship-related. We were able to identify specific action steps of change he could take. He took some of them. He felt better. We never focused.

Client C: After several years of therapy with me in which he has made job-related and relationship-related changes for the better in his life, he now mostly comes in and sits in silence for all or the greater part of our session. This has been going on for about a year now.

A couple times a month I ask him whether these sessions are continuing to be helpful to him. I do not ask what he does in them. He tells me they are continuing to be helpful.

I have a sense of what I think may be going on. Nothing in his life has ever been fully his. In previous therapies, the therapist was always the one guiding the process. He wants something to be his and his alone. That is what our time together is. Why should I interrupt it?

When I shared with him this interpretation of what was going on for him in the therapy, he agreed that this is what has been going on for him in the therapy. Then, he went back to staring out the window, reflectively.

♦

In conclusion, I would say that my aim in therapy is to give a therapeutic response. A therapeutic response is one that helps the client. Help can take many different forms. An experiential response is one very special kind of therapeutic response. It is very powerful. Focusing and listening are specific methods that provide an experiential response and thus facilitate client movement. They are not the *only* ways to get such movement. Nor is such a response the *only* kind of response that is therapeutic. Where Gendlin says that focusing is what successful clients do in therapy I would prefer to say that focusing is *one* of the things successful clients may do in therapy. Focusing is very powerful and not always necessary.

So long as I keep the words in the above paragraph in mind, I can make a great deal of good use of Gendlin's approach to therapy. I recommend it as an excellent starting place for any therapist. It orients one to a person-centered therapy delivered in a focusing-oriented manner.

Three

The Therapeutic Relationship

In two places in Focusing-Oriented Psychotherapy, Gendlin makes it explicit that the therapist-client interaction is of primary importance in FOT. He says that "interpersonal interaction (between therapist and client) is the most important therapeutic avenue. Its quality affects all the other avenues, because they all happen within the interaction" (1996, 283). Later, in the same chapter he provides this guideline for FOT: "In therapy, the relationship…is of first importance, listening is second, and focusing instructions come only third" (1996, 297).

That is about as explicit a statement as can be made about the importance of the therapeutic relationship. It comes first. Everything else depends upon it. Its quality is of first importance. The relationship's importance comes even before the specific techniques for which Gendlin is known.

Unfortunately, these statements do not appear until the next to the last chapter in a dense and difficult book. I do not know what proportion of readers actually gets there. There is no foreshadowing earlier in the book of this most important point. Perhaps that is why sometimes Gendlin's work is portrayed as not being aware enough of and responsive to the therapeutic relationship.

What does Gendlin have to say about the therapeutic relationship?

First, he makes clear what he means by the relationship: "The experienced relationship is bodily felt and concrete; it is not what is said about the relationship. Neither is it how the two people perceive or think of each other. The relationship is each time the concretely ongoing interaction" (ibid., 284).

I think that here Gendlin is trying to make use of the fact that talking about the relationship did not correlate with outcome in an early piece of research out of which the focusing method came. No *content* correlated with outcome. What was talked about in therapy did not matter. How anything was talked about did matter. Gendlin is distancing himself somewhat here from Rogers who did put emphasis on how the client perceived the relationship as indicated by how often he talked about it (Rogers 1951).

Gendlin goes on to identify what he calls "The Most Common Untherapeutic Interaction" and follows that by some statements about what he thinks the interaction ought to be like.

The Most Common Untherapeutic Interaction is the kind where the therapist tells and the client is told to. The client is passive and the therapist is active. This kind of activity is the therapist acting like an expert authority who has to tell the client things about himself: "In therapy the interaction should not too often duplicate the common childhood type in which someone defines the reality for the client and the client is supposed to listen (and obey)" (ibid., 285). This superordinate/subordinate role structure too often mirrors the very kinds of interactions that have brought the client to therapy. They cannot fix that of which they are further examples.

So what ought the therapeutic relationship be like?

Gendlin has his own vocabulary about this:

• "Putting Nothing Between"

Gendlin writes that when he is expecting a client he needs to "put my own feelings and concerns to one side. I don't put them far, because I need to sense when something registers there. I also put aside theories and procedures, all that I have discussed so far in this book. All that is on the side. In front of me the space is free, ready for the other person"(ibid., 286).

I had a beautiful lesson about this one time when I came early for my session with Gendlin. I always felt slightly annoyed that when I saw him there would be notebooks and pieces of paper on the outskirts of the area between us. I would sit on a sofa and he in a chair across from me. There was nothing in between.

When I came early and Gendlin was having a smoke while I went upstairs I saw all those notebooks and pieces of paper lying between the sofa and the chair! By the time I came out of the bathroom, they had been moved to the periphery of the area. There was nothing in between.

That is how literal Gendlin's words are.

- "The Person in There"

Gendlin relates to whom he calls "the person in there". This is the person struggling to get out from under all the gunk that is in the way. It is the healthy person buried inside all the neurosis. Gendlin always looks for that person, even when he is hardly present: "When a client reports having no self, being dead or absent inside, I say "I know there is a *you* way under there, and we won't stop till we find it" (ibid., 288).

- "Providing Safety"

Gendlin writes that he considers the therapy relationship as one between "two real people" in which there is a frame to provide safety for the client:

> The client needs to be free and safe to express all feelings. The safety requires that the therapist will not act in response to a client's feelings of sexual attraction, or a client's report of unlawful behavior…To keep this safety unshakable is part of the reality of a therapy relationship. The world offers many sexual opportunities, and there are also a great many police. The therapy relationship is rare and has another purpose. This makes it narrower in acceptable conduct, but deeper than most other relationships (ibid., 289).

At this point Gendlin turns from the successful therapeutic relation-ship to what the therapist is to do when the relationship is, as he says, off-kilter. He is quite definite here: "If something is out of kilter in the relationship it must be straightened out before any other therapeutic means can be expected to have good effects" (p.292).

Unlike Rogers, Gendlin admits the possibility of transference (p.294). He also recommends that the therapist be aware of his own feeling reactions to his client's way of being at any particular moment and to use these as clues to what may be going on in the moment for the client. The therapist may actually need to express some of his feel-ing reactions to the client. Gendlin is chary here. He accepts this as a possibility rather than embracing it as sometimes crucial.

I think it is fair to say that Gendlin could have said more about the specifics of his way of using the therapeutic relationship, but he is clear that the therapeutic relationship is primary to the success of therapy. The positioning of the chapter on the relationship as the next-to-last chapter in the book is unfortunate.

◆

In underlining the importance of the therapeutic relationship Gendlin is in good company.

For this chapter I have reviewed several edited books on research in psychotherapy (Miller, Duncan, and Hubble 1997; Hubble, Duncan, and Miller 1999; Norcross 2002; Nathan and Gorman 2002; Cain and Seeman 2001; Bergin and Garfield 1971; Gurman and Razin 1977).

There is overwhelming evidence that the therapeutic relationship, its quality, the strength of the alliance between therapist and client really does affect the outcome of therapy. The following testimonials are from psychologists who have done extensive reviews of the research literature.

- "It seems beyond doubt that a positive therapeutic relationship is a necessary (but probably not sufficient) component of all forms of effective psychotherapy" (in Hubble, Duncan, and Miller, Eds. 1999, 161).

- "The therapy relationship…makes substantial and consistent contributions to psychotherapeutic outcome independent of the specific type of treatment" (Norcross 2002, 441).
- "*the quality of the interpersonal context* is the sine qua non in all forms of therapy" (Strupp 1995, 70, emphasis in the original in Miller, Duncan, and Hubble 1997, 27).
- "From his extensive research on therapy Michael Lambert has concluded that at least 30% of the outcome of therapy is based upon the therapeutic relationship. This makes it more robust than *any* specific method is in its effect on the outcome of therapy" (Lambert as cited in Miller, Duncan, and Hubble, op.cit., 27).
- "Relationship factors make up the second largest contributor to change in therapy. The client's view of the relationship is the "trump" card in therapy outcome, second only to the winning hand of the client's strengths. Clients who rate the relationship highly are very likely to be successful in achieving their goals. Despite how chronic, intractable, or 'impossible' a case may appear change is more likely to occur, if the client's view of the relationship is favorable" (Hubble, Duncan, and Miller 1999, 412).

Older theories and studies point in the same direction.

- Carl Rogers wrote that "in a wide variety of professional work involving relationships with people…it is the *quality* of the interpersonal encounter with the client which is the most significant element in determining effectiveness"(1962, 157, his italics).
- In 1936 Saul Rosenzweig published his brief but seminal paper on "the common factors" that lead to therapeutic change (Rosenzweig 1936). The therapeutic relationship is one of the most important of these.
- "Whitehorn and Betz's now classic contribution was a retrospective study of seven psychiatrists who had an improvement rate of 75 per cent in their schizophrenic patients as contrasted to seven other psy-

chiatrists of similar training who had an improvement rate of only 27 per cent…the successful therapists were warm and attempted to understand the patient in a personal, immediate and idiosyncratic way; whereas the less successful therapists tended to relate to the patient in a more impersonal manner, focusing upon psychopathology and a more external kind of understanding" (Truax and Mitchell in Bergin and Garfield 1971, 302).

It is unfortunate that research upon the relationship has used so many different kinds of variables and definitions of what is being studied (e.g. the therapeutic alliance, the necessary and sufficient conditions for therapeutic success) that more specific statements about the optimal therapeutic relationship remain in competition with each other. There is no absolutely correct summing-up statement of what in the relationship leads in the direction of client progress. Not enough of the variables used in these studies have been truly interactional variables rather than therapist variables or client variables. Nevertheless, it seems to me beyond a shadow of a doubt that the quality of the therapeutic relationship is primary to the outcome of any particular instance of psychotherapy.

◆

When I had gotten to this point which was to be the end point of my chapter on the therapeutic relationship, I found in my inveterate journal keeping a sentence that leaped out at me. The sentence was "In therapy I give people a deep experience of human caring." I do not feel that I have said enough yet about this aspect of the therapeutic relationship and so will do so here.

Gendlin says that the therapist-client relationship is of first importance, but I do not think that the word 'love" appears in his index. (I just checked. It doesn't.) Gendlin does not do justice to the importance of certain therapist attitudes in affecting the quality of the relationship and hence the outcome of therapy. The therapist needs to cherish, to prize, to love the client. The client needs to feel loved. Not, of course, in the romantic sense. I am talking *agape* here, not *eros.*

Billy Kwan, the androgynous hunchback-hero of the movie The Year of Living Dangerously pecks out on his typewriter the phrases: "What must be done? What must be done? One must give love to whomever God has put in one's path."

Of course, seldom do we find the therapist who can live up to such an ideal. I do not. Not by a long shot. I can come to love most clients ("the person in there"). It is better to turn some people away. Yet, even if we consider unconditional love to be an asymptotic goal that the therapist can only approach, it is just this that ought to be our goal. Maybe love is not enough…but it sure goes a long way.

In a touching scene from the play, *Agnes of God*, the therapist tells the patient (played by Amanda Plummer) that she loves her. Agnes looks up and asks her, "Do you really or are you just pretending?" She thus puts into words the doubt that many of our clients have of us. Is it for real? Are we for real?

This is a crucial moment No role-playing of a Freudian or early Rogerian kind of neutrality will serve the therapist here. Nor will reframing. Nor will interpreting. Nor will anything having to do with rapid eye movements or neuro-linguistic programming.

The therapist must step up to the plate. The therapist must answer the question. The answer must be truthful and genuine and transparent. The love must be for real.

So…remember this in what follows: I am almost presuming that the therapist will endeavor to love his/her client and will know that that is as important as anything else. Better yet, strike that 'endeavor'. The therapist will love the client. If this does happen, the rest may very well take care of itself. If it does not happen there may be some therapeutic progress but not of the thorough and lasting kind in which I am most interested. The knowledge of methods and skills that you will find in the rest of this book can be of help. It needs be undertaken in a spirit of unconditional love for "the person in there".

Part Two:

Focusing and Listening

Focusing and Listening are the key methods in Focusing-Oriented Therapy. The following essays introduce each of them and then show something about how they can be combined.

Four

Focusing

Growing up, August was my favorite month of the year. My family spent the month at the seashore in Atlantic City, New Jersey.

This was the old Atlantic City, long before the casinos took over. We ate out every night. We walked the boardwalk. We visited the arcades. We played pokerino, skee-ball, and miniature golf.

And—best of all—we spent every sunny day at the beach.

I had an ocean ritual that never varied:

We are at the beach by 10 a.m. I run immediately full-speed into the ocean. I get into about four feet of water. I throw myself head-first into the water.

Thud, splash.

I stay underwater for as long as I can. I come up for air. I shake my hair out of my eyes. I look around. I take in the scene: the seagulls, other bathers, the blueness of the blue sky. I take in the panoramic view only after my total immersion in the salty Atlantic.

Focusing is our ocean. I am going to throw us right into it. I am going to present one person's full round of focusing step-by-step. After, we will step back, shake the water out of our eyes, and take an overview of focusing.

◆

In what follows I am the guide. My client is the focuser. I guide the focuser through the eight steps in which I now teach a round of focusing.

This focuser is quite experienced. He is a virtuoso of his affective life. He is a social worker and a poet. He has come to me for focusing-oriented therapy. This is our twenty-second session. It was tape-recorded. The date is November 12, 1997.[1]

The focuser is sitting in a light tan upholstered chair across from me and to my left. He takes his glasses off and perches them somewhat precariously on the corner of my glass-top table which stands to my left and his right.

In what follows my *focusing instructions* and *listening responses* are in *italics*. His responses and any other comments by me are in regular type-face. The words not spoken—my names for the eight steps—are in **bold face**.

He is ready to jump in. He closes his eyes.

I begin guiding:

G: **1. Saying hello**: *Find a comfortable position…Relax and close your eyes…Take a few deep breaths…and when you're ready just ask, "How am I inside right now?" Don't answer. Give an answer time to form in your body…Turn your attention like a searchlight into your inside feeling place and just greet whatever you find there…Practice taking a friendly attitude toward whatever is there…(30 seconds of silence)*

F: There is a good feeling—pride—in my chest area. It is about the poem I just finished.

G: *You feel pride in your just-finished poem and the physical feeling is in your chest area.*

F: Yes.

G: Do you want to stay with the feeling or clear a space?[2]

F: Clear a space.

G: **2. Clearing a space…Making a list (optional)**: *Now, imagine yourself sitting on a park bench. Ask yourself, "What's in the way between me and feeling all fine right now?" Let whatever comes up, come up. Don't go inside any particular thing right now. Just stack* *each thing at a comfortable distance from you on the bench...Take inventory: "What's between me and feeling all fine right now?" [or "What are the main things..."] If the list stops, ask, "Except for that am I all fine?" If more comes up, add it to the stack. Stay distanced from your stack. Give me a signal when you're ready for the next step.*

F: I want to acknowledge the good feeling again.

G: Yes, yes. Please do.

F: And now I want to look at...the stuff on the bench.

G: Yeah.

F: One imperfect line in the poem...

G: Put that on the bench.

F: My fear about money, about having enough to live on.

G: Put that out there.

F: Sadness about aging...my adopted child...and my wife's withdrawal from me...(Big sigh) That is about it right now.

G: *So there is...the imperfect line from the poem, the fear about money, sadness about—*

F: Growing older.

G: *—growing older...and the adopted child and...your wife's withdrawal from you.*

F: Yes. (Thirty seconds pause)

G: **3. Picking a problem** *Now, feel yourself as if magnetically pulled toward the one thing in your stack that most needs your attention right now...If you have any trouble letting it choose you, ask, "What is worst?" (or, "What is best?"—good feelings can be worked with too!)..."What most needs some work right now?"..."What won't let go of me?"...Pick one thing. (short pause): Now, feel—*

F: Our child...Maya.

G: Ok. (pause: twenty seconds) Ready to move on?

F: Yes.

G: **4. Letting the felt sense form**: *Now ask, "What does this whole thing feel like?"..."What is the whole feel of it?" Don't answer with what you already know about it. Listen to your body...Sense the issue* *freshly...Give your body 30 seconds to a minute for the feel of "all of that" to form.*

F: (one minute silence; then begins to cry) I DON'T FEEL LIKE SHE IS MINE...She is some...foreign...kid living in our house...I mean, she's Indian...but that isn't the foreign I mean...I have a sick feeling about her in my insides...in my middle.

G: *Sick feeling in the middle. (F: Yes.) She is foreign to you and it isn't the Indian-ness that is the foreign.*

F: Yes.

G: You may have already done this step but let's just check...**5. Finding the handle:** *Find a word, phrase, image, sound or gesture that feels like it matches, comes from, or will act as a handle on the felt sense, the whole feel of it. Keep your attention on the area in your body where you feel it, and just let a word, phrase, image, sound or gesture appear that feels like a good fit.*[3]

F: The handle is 'foreign.' She is like a stranger to me (long pause)...so is her mother, I mean, my wife. She's so distant.

G: So the child is foreign to you like a stranger and your wife is—

F: Cold.

G: *Cold...you are out in the cold vis-a-vis both of them and the feeling is in the middle of your body.*
      Let's just check all that...
      6. Resonating the handle: *Say the word, phrase, image, sound or gesture back to yourself...Check it against your body...See if there is a sense of "rightness," an inner "yes, that's it"...If there isn't, gently let go of that handle and let one that fits better appear.*

F: The handle is right...It is now about both of them...I mean, and me. It is important that it is BOTH of them. Yeah. That gives me a little shift inside.

G: *The "both" gives you a little shift.*

F: Yes.

G: **7. Asking and receiving:** *Now we are going to ask the felt sense some questions. Some it will answer. Some it won't. Receive whatever*

answers it gives. Ask the questions with an expectantly friendly atti-
tude and be receptive to whatever it sends you.
Ask, "What's the crux of this feeling?" "What's the main thing about
it?" Don't answer with your head; let the body feeling answer.

F: (after thirty seconds) I've never felt like I belonged any-
     where…not even in my own family of origin.

G: Not even—

F: No.

G: *And ask, "What's the worst of this feeling?" "What makes it so bad?"*
     Wait…

F: It is the "anywhere"…I've never belonged anywhere.

G: *The worst is the never having belonged "anywhere."*
     And ask, "What's wrong?" Imagine the felt sense as a shy child sit-
     ting on a stoop. It needs caring encouragement to speak. Go over to it,
     sit down, and gently ask, "What's wrong?" Wait…

F: (talks slowly, with pauses, some effort to get the words) I've
     always wanted to belong…and no one has ever 'belonged' me.

G: *You've yearned…but no one has ever 'belonged' you.*

F: Yeah.

G: *And ask, "What does this feeling need?"*

F: It needs to feel like I do belong somewhere.

G: *That you do belong somewhere…*
     And now ask, "What is a good small step in the right direction for this
     thing?" "What is a step in the direction of fresh air?"

F: I just got an image of moving my chair right into the circle…not
     sitting outside…alone.

G: *A good small step is moving your chair into the circle.*

F: Yes…that's interesting.

G: Something interesting there…(I pause for thirty seconds to see
     if he has more to say. He does not and so I go on.)
     Ask, "What needs to happen?" "What actions need to be taken?"

F: Moving the chair into…

G: Moving the chair into…

F: The circle.

G: The circle.

And now ask, "What would my body feel like if this thing were all bet-ter, all resolved?" Move your body into the position or posture it would be in if this were all cleared up. This is called looking the answer up in the back of the book. Now, from this position, ask, "What's between me and here?" "What's in the way of it being all Ok?" Wait…

F: You know…there is a space in the circle…like it is waiting there for me…and I'm the one who isn't…joining. They're not keep-ing me out. I'm keeping me out.

G: So if this thing were all better…

F: No. No. I didn't follow your instructions.

G: Oh. Ok. I see.

F: It is the truth of how it is right now.

G: Oh, I see…The issue shifted.

F: Yes.

G: *It is you who doesn't join rather than them keeping you out.*

F: Yes! (strong affirmation; pause)

G: *Finally, ask your felt sense space to send you the exactly right focus-ing question you need at this moment…Now ask the felt sense that question. Don't answer with your head. Just hang out with the felt sense, keep it company, let it respond. Wait…*

F: I want to make sure…'Why am I not in the circle?' (chuckles) Because I keep myself out of it. It's a habit. Brilliant! Just bril-liant! (laughing) I'd rather bitch, moan, and complain…HA! HA! HA!

G: What? (I'm not sure what 'HA! HA! HA!' refers to.)

F: Don't you see?

G: Not yet.

F: It is all MAYA. (Hindu term for illusion) (He breaks into tears for a few minutes.) It is a good name for her…yes it is…but it is 'my maya.'

G: You like her name…

F: It fits.

G: *The name fits…but it is your maya.*

F: You got it.

G: *(A summary statement) Your maya is that THEY keep you out.*

F: YES (a strong YES affirming that he feels really heard and understood).

G: **8. Coming back**: *Ok, now you have a minute to use however you'd like. Some people find it useful to retrace the steps they've come. Some like to stretch and relax. Some find it useful to underline the furthest place they've come to; pitch a tent there so you can come back to it if you want…Use this minute however you would like and then open your eyes…and this round of focusing is over.*

F: (Yawns…stretches hands over head…shakes out torso…opens eyes…puts on glasses.) That was quite a trip!

◆

Focusing is quite a trip.

As you have just seen, for me, a *focusing round* in its entirety is an eight-step process through which a guide leads a focuser, who usually has his/her eyes closed.

Let us look back now at this example to see what it teaches us about the focusing process.

First, notice what I, the guide, do and don't do.

Mostly I give *focusing instructions* and *listening responses*.

My focusing instructions are printed in an appendix at the end of this book. There are different types of instructions (e.g., Gendlin 1981; Cornell 1996). No set of instructions is sacred. It is good to experience a few different sets and see what works best for you. My set is simply the instructions that I use now. It has evolved over time. I like these instructions. They have worked well for me.

I will take up listening in more detail in the next chapter. For now, let me just say that a listening response is an attempt to say back to another person the felt essence of what he or she has just said. Listening is a way of showing one has understood what has been said. It is a way of keeping a person company.

Now, note what I do not do as the guide. I do not interpret, give advice, fix the problem, tell my own story, or give a mini-lecture on what it is like for a couple to adopt an Indian child. I take pains not to in any way, no matter how subtle, *mangle* the focuser's process.

I give focusing instructions and listening responses.

And I do other things too: I keep pointing out the bodily nature of the experiencing ("the physical feeling is in your chest area"); I reinforce the focuser's wanting to acknowledge the good feeling again ("Yes, yes. Please do."). I notice and verbalize when a 'shift' has occurred. ("The 'both' gives you a shift.") I am happy when the focuser ignores my instructions and does something better for himself. ("Oh, I see…The issue shifted.") When I don't understand something that seems important ("HA! HA! HA!"), I ask for clarification. And I allow myself a summary statement that stays very close to the focuser's own formulation ("your maya is that **they** keep you out").

Let us look now at the focuser.

What does he do? He stays on track. He does not go off into intellectualizing, explaining, friendly chit chat, tangents, or obsessive ruminations. Had he done any of these—as all focusers sometimes do—I would have gently brought him back to what he is doing now—focusing.

The example does not show that this focuser has already at times 'dealt' with the adoption issue in therapy. He has talked *about* this issue in earlier sessions. He has *inferred* various things about it ("It must be that"). He has offered various interpretations of his behavior ("I don't get closer to her probably because…"). And he has gone over some hand-me-down answers about feeling like his kid is a stranger to him ("My wife says…").

This is important. So many people, so much of the time, give what I would call "hand-me down" answers to issues in therapy. They say what their last therapist said or their older brother or their best friend or some guru or the latest self-help book, or Oprah.

But in focusing I ask the client to do something radically different: to approach the issue freshly, to experience it directly here and now, to let it talk to him from inside him. This difference is basic to focusing and helps explain what is so therapeutic about focusing—as opposed to obsessing, criticizing, passing on others' answers, etc.

In the example above when the issue is approached directly via focusing…it changes in content, and there are changes in the focuser's bodily state. First, it is not just the child who is foreign, but his wife is far from him too. The recognition that it is 'both' begins to let something move—shift—in his body. More happens. He did not belong in his family of origin. He has never belonged anywhere. And then: it is **he** not **they** who are keeping him out now. This last is a major new insight that is accompanied by a physical release—laughing. In a way that is usual for focusing but is particularly dramatic in this example, the problem has mutated (Gendlin 1964). At the end of the session he recognizes that he has come a long way. He sees the matter differently (insight) and he feels better (felt shift).

◆

It is time to step back from this example and get an overview of focusing.

Focusing is a quiet, direct, affective, eyes-closed sensing into one's bodily experiencing to find one's whole FELT SENSE of a problem, issue, or situation and, through asking the felt sense questions, to achieve one or more FELT SHIFTS, bodily resolutions of the matter.

Let me say all that over as it is so central to everything else:

Focusing invitations lead the focuser towards the bodily felt sense of a something, a something that is at first vague and fuzzy or murky. Through focusing this "something" gets clearer and gets symbolized. The symbol may be a word, phrase, image, sound or gesture. No one kind of symbol is better than any other kind. The symbol is checked against the bodily felt experiencing. When the symbol is accurate there is a beginning felt shift. The felt sense is then asked in a friendly way open-ended questions so as to bring new insights and physiological release and a feeling of well-being.

Focusing is a process of finding felt senses, being friendly to them, symbolizing them, and allowing them to shift. A self-propelled feeling process carries forward the focuser's experiencing until a stopping place is reached. One half-hour of continuous focusing is a lot.

Focusing was developed in the 1960s by Eugene Gendlin partly out of his philosophy of experiencing (1962) and partly out of research on the process and outcome of psychotherapy (1961, 1967, 1981). In the research Gendlin asked, 'What distinguishes successful from unsuccessful therapy?' He found that it was not what clients talked about. Research showed that the *content* of the sessions did not distinguish successful from unsuccessful therapy. Nor was it the orientation of the therapist. Rather, it was *how* the clients talked. Those clients who spoke from their own *experiencing process* were more likely to profit from their therapy than those who did not.

Gendlin then reasoned that if we know what clients have to do to profit from therapy—make symbols for their own experiencing process—can we teach people how to do this? From this question Gendlin crystallized out and then refined the technique of focusing. Focusing is a precise specification of what successful clients do in therapy. They focus. They know how to make touch with a conceptually vague but bodily felt sense. They stay with it. They let unexpected stuff emerge from it. The ability to focus correlates with success in psychotherapy (Hendricks 2002).

For forty years now Gendlin has been teaching people how to focus. His book, Focusing, has sold over 500,000 copies and has been translated into fifteen languages. He and his followers have given focusing workshops around the world. The 2006 Membership Directory of the Focusing Institute lists over 10,000 members in thirty-seven countries.

♦

As we have seen, focusing is a skill that a guide teaches to a focuser. As I teach it, it proceeds in steps. We have seen a complete round of focusing including all eight steps as I now teach them.

Focusing is an aesthetically appealing but subtly nuanced and difficult-to-be-completely-grasped process. Examples help teach it. Here are some. I will share with you five examples of focusing for self-help and five examples of focusing in therapy. Each example illuminates one or more aspects of the focusing process.

The first example comes from Gendlin's book, FOCUSING. It is my favorite example from that book. In it, what is being focused upon is a troubling incident, the kind of thing with which clients sometimes start therapy sessions. Here it is being worked upon for self-help.

The example illustrates particularly well both the 'clearing a space' movement of focusing and the changing and deepening of an issue when focusing is applied to it.

In the example, Peggy works part-time. Her husband John comes home one evening jubilant. His bank has plans to promote him. In his excitement, he knocks a piece of Peggy's china off the table. It breaks. Peggy flies into a rage, refuses to cook dinner, and runs upstairs in tears:

> She was surprised and upset by her…outburst. Stormy scenes were not usual for her. So she focused…
>
> She began by getting as comfortable as possible, removing all unnecessary physical irritations that might have masked what her body wanted to tell her. She washed her face because it felt hot and itchy after crying. She took off her shoes, propped a pillow against the headboard of the bed, and leaned back against it.
>
> She stacked all her problems to one side, as though making a space for herself in a jumbled storage room. "Why don't I feel terrific right now? Well, there's that big pile of dog-eared school papers I still have to finish. And there's that problem about Jeff getting sent home from kindergarten. And of course there is this lousy new thing about the broken dish."
>
> **The felt sense**. Now she let her attention go to the problem that, at the moment, seemed to be the worst: the stormy scene involving that broken dish.
>
> She asked, "What does **all that** feel like?" and then she let the unclear sense come to her in its own way—large, vague,

formless at first, lacking words to describe it, lacking labels or identifying marks of any kind.

Finding a handle. Now, very gently, she asked what the quality of the felt sense was. She tried to let the felt sense name itself, or to let an image come and fit it.

She had asked: "What is the worst of this?" The feeling came, "Anger at John." A further question: "Over the broken dish?" The wordless reply, "No. The dish has hardly anything to do with it. The anger is over his air of jubilation, the way he radiates confidence about his future."

Thus did the problem change. The inner shift was unmistakable. She received this fully and sensed it over and over, feeling the change going on in her body. When her body had finished changing, she went on....

Again, she got the felt sense, the changed way the whole problem was in her body at this moment. "His jubilation. What now is the **whole sense** of that?"

Resonating. She took the word "jealous" and checked it against the felt sense. "Jealous, is that the right word? Is that what this sense is?" The felt sense and the word apparently were a close match, but not a perfect one. It seemed that the felt sense said, "This isn't exactly jealousy. There's jealousy in it somewhere, but—"

She tried "sort-of-jealous" and got a tiny movement and the breath that let her know that was right enough, as a handle on the felt sense. She did it again, and...yes.

Asking. Now she asked the felt sense itself: "What is this sort-of-jealous? What about the whole problem makes this sort-of-jealous?"

She let the question reach the unclear felt sense, and it stirred slightly. "What is **that**?" she asked, almost wordlessly. And then, abruptly, the shift came. "Sort-of-jealous...uh...it's more like...a feeling of **being left behind**."

"Ah!" That "ah!" came with a large, satisfying sense of movement. Peggy's body was telling her that she was unhappy over the fact that her own career was stalled.

But this quality—the feeling of being left behind—was only the tip of the iceberg. Peggy wanted to see if it could lead to more change and movement.

And so she went through the cycle of focusing movements again. "What is this left-behind feeling? What's really in it for me? What's the worst of it?"

This focusing session lasted for perhaps 20 minutes. When it was over, Peggy felt enormously refreshed. The shape of her problem had changed, and **she** had changed. She and John then talked calmly about their lives and their futures. The broken dish was forgotten.

That one focusing session had not made Peggy's motherhood versus career problem vanish, but it had started a series of beneficial changes inside her. Further sessions told her more about herself and helped her to move from where she was stuck (Gendlin 1981, 46-50).

Notice that through focusing Peggy has used an everyday experience as a teacher. She does not have to keep reacting to broken dishes. She gets the message.

Here is the self-focusing session of an advanced student:

She has had breast cancer and a round of chemo.

In the transcript that follows she is focusing alone. She is both the focuser and the guide. I have put my minimal commentary in parentheses.

Focusing/Writing October, 2006

Guide: Do you want to clear a space?

Focuser: I don't need to. I know exactly where I need to go.

G: Okay, so just go there. Good. Just breathe.

F: This is hard. I found out that my cancer marker number is up again. It scared the shit out of me. (It is a sign that she still has cancer in her body.) I'm better now but I was really a wreck.

G: A wreck?

F: Actually, I was really just anxious. Scared, really scared. At the time it felt like a death sentence. Now I'm more balanced. It's up nine points from its lowest point. But only three points out of normal range. There's still cancer, but it's not at a detectable level. But it's still fucking THERE.

G: So can you get a feel for the whole of it?

(This proves to be an excellent intervention. Just see what happens…)

F: It's easier to get a feel for the parts of it: the cancer and me having cancer.

G: Which one do you want to start with?

F: The cancer. It's insidious, stealthy, and relentless. Truly an enemy—but a primitive kind of enemy. Not like a psychopathic killer (organized type). More like a cockroach: able to defeat science's most sophisticated attempts to eradicate it. That's more of a handle than a felt sense.

(Notice how she goes from the handle to the felt sense.)

F: The felt sense is of having microscopic cockroach eggs floating around in my bloodstream.

(Is she really feeling this or is it really another handle?)

G: It's visceral—

F: It's visceral. A feeling of panic and powerlessness about having contaminated blood

G: It sounds like you are getting to the felt sense of having cancer.

F: Yes. Initially the feeling was terror, an 'oh shit, no" feeling. It felt like doom, a death sentence. With more discussion with my Alternative Health doctor I've calmed down. Now it's more of a hopeful alertness with tinges of fear. *The image I get is of a love letter, burnt around the edges.* That is the handle. That image makes me cry. I don't even know what it means or why it came to me but it really seems to be the handle for my felt sense of me with cancer still/again.

(Notice that she does not consciously know what the image means but she is exactly clear that this is the handle on the felt sense. The touch-tone is not intellectual meaning).

I'm ready to go on.

G: Oh, sorry. Do you want questions now?

F: Yes.

G: Okay. What's the worst of all this?

F: Worst? The worst is not knowing. No, maybe not. The worst is the risk; it may be one of those strains of cockroach eggs you can't stomp out no matter how hard you try, no matter how vigilant you are. I will have a better idea of that in another month. Actually, there's a certain protection in not knowing. For the moment at least it is not like a death sentence.

G: What would it be like if it were all better?

F: My life would be a love letter with no burnt edges.

G: What does it need?

F: Hmmm. I think I already have most of what I need: a terrific doctor, a plan for therapeutic alternatives to try, wonderful support and love. What more could I ask for? I know. Discipline. The discipline to stay with the various regimens…Actually the cancer diet is the only weak link. I already do the rest…Also, I need to be patient with myself and with the process. Everything takes time. At least twice as long as I think it should.

G: Where is the fresh air?

F: I'm living my life. I'm feeling better.

G: What is a small step?

F: Actually, a big step. Going to Smith farm for a seven-day retreat. Spending a week sharing with other cancer survivors…I need that.

Here is another *self-help* example.

Maria and Lawrence have just formed a focusing partnership. They have taken a workshop with Gene Gendlin and practiced focusing under supervision from me seven times. It is a Tuesday in the Spring of 1987. This is their fourteenth meeting:

L: You want to be the guide or the focuser?

M: I'll focus. I really need it today.

L: Ok. Close your eyes. Bring your attention into your body. See what is there.

M: It is like I am crying and screaming inside.

L: Crying and screaming…Do you want to put things out on the bench? (Notice the option.)

M: No. I'll stick with where I am…It just changed!

L: So, what is the whole feel of—

M: Now, I want to shake and throttle him.

L: Shake and throttle—

M: My fucking father! He wouldn't send me a penny towards the down payment on the new house.

L: He wouldn't send you a—

M: I'm really pissed.

L: Yes, you are! Is there a question you want to ask the "pissed"?

M: (Much more slowly) Yes…A couple: Do I deserve the money?…Do I need the money?

L: So ask your inside feeling place, "Do you deserve the money? Do you need the money?"

M: (deep silence; then, laughter)

L: Something is funny.

M: I don't **need** his money. I just wanted to get his goat. I **wanted** him to turn me down—again—so I could feel self-righteous (laughing).

L: There seems to have been a felt shift (understatement).

M: You know it! God, I'm still playing that game with him. The game of "punished-unjustly brat." Enough of that!

L: That **is** different.

M: Yes, it is. Let me take a bathroom break. Then it is your turn. Thanks.

Notice how Lawrence reflects back to Maria the emotional essence of what she has said and then may give her a focusing direction. Maria's speech starts quickly, slows down (typical of focusing) and her "crying and screaming" turn first into quiet and then laughter. Her whole sense of what is going on changes radically as does her feeling state.

Just as the "Peggy" example is my favorite from FOCUSING, this next is my favorite from FOCUSING-ORIENTED PSYCHOTHERAPY. Gendlin says it is an instance when in order to explain focusing he turned to doing it. He is on the radio. The interviewer (who becomes the focuser) is the talk show host. The example deals only with finding the felt sense. Why do I consider it so important? The interviewer brings up two subjects—race and condominium prices—which a socio-politically oriented therapist might readily latch onto. Gendlin recognizes that these can be important factors. But, by staying with finding the truly felt sense, he helps the interviewer find what is true for him right now. They do not go off on an ideologically fueled but not-felt tangent:

Interviewer: I'm having trouble understanding, and I think our audience probably does too,what this unclear felt sense is, that you talk about.

Gendlin: Well, if you would be willing, choose some problem of your own, for a minute. You need not say what it is, just pick one in your mind.

I: That's easy. I'm right in one. My building is being turned into condominiums, and we have to move. It makes me so angry. That whole way of squeezing people's money out of them—so very much money for just an apartment—and that whole policy is wrong. We're black, of course, and that has something to do with it too. And I *hate* moving. Everything is disrupted. I'm just not ready to move.

G: I know that this is a big issue, about condominiums, and I know we could talk about that for a long time. I can understand that you're angry about it. And the race issue that comes into it is even bigger, I know. But I'll ask you, so I can explain focusing, to do something a little different. Could you just sense the whole of your discomfort now, about that whole moving business, and—just as if you didn't know about it already—sense how it makes you feel. See if you can get one word or phrase for *the quality* of it.

I: Well, I know what I feel. I'm not ready. I'm not prepared for it. It comes as a surprise; I didn't expect it.

G: Just be with the sense of "not prepared." You know a lot of what that means, but just as if you didn't know it, just stay a little while with that uncomfortable sense, that you're calling "not prepared."

(Silence…it seemed like a long silence because this was on the radio, but it lasted perhaps 15 seconds.)

G: Probably this is hard to do, right now, you're having to run the program and so forth, but we're only explaining to the audience how this is done, maybe later when you have a quiet minute—

I: (Laughs)

G: Why are you laughing?

I: *I've got it. It answered me. I know what it is. It came.*
G: Now, you don't need to say what it is.
I: Oh, I can say it. It's being middle-aged. That's what it is.
G: Oh—
I: I'm not prepared to carry heavy things. What are the women going to say when that comes out? I'm afraid I'll hurt my back. We haven't moved for years, and I haven't done any heavy carrying for 20 years. I am sure going to look foolish. But, of course, that's nothing. It's getting middle-aged, that's what bothers me. We can move.

(Relief shows on the interviewer's face.)

Notice that in getting the feel of the whole of it, the whole problem changes, and there is some relief.

Gendlin comments: "I…want to be clear that I am not trivializing problems about condominiums and certainly not about race. This processing step does not in any way diminish the seriousness that this man feels about social questions. [But] what exactly had this man not known before that he now knows? It…was not the well-known disruption of moving that made him feel 'not ready, not prepared.' It was rather his being middle-aged that came there when he let the murky sense give the next step" (Gendlin 1996, 95).

The murky felt sense, when attended to, tells us what our experienced difficulties are right now. Without the felt sense we can intellectualize forever. We can talk about our issues obsessively and endlessly. We can clothe ourselves in other people's certainties about what is wrong—or right—with us. We can obsess to our confused self's delight. We can go round and round and get nowhere.

Or, we can use focusing and go inside and directly experience 'the rub' of it. Only then can we say that we truly know what is there. All the rest is commentary.

One more example of self-help focusing just came to me. I am the focuser. My journal is my companion. I am guiding myself. Something happened inside me as I finished writing the previous example:

The feeling is heavy, like, in my gut and in my arms...like 'heavy lifting'...the guy in the example...something in common between him and me and how I'm feeling about this paper.

(I'm quiet, eyes closed, waiting.)

It is about being middle-aged.

What is 'middle-aged' about the paper?

Oh, I'm taking something I wrote in my forties (Friedman 1986) and revising it now in my sixtieth year. I feel *nostalgic* for when I originally wrote it...*that time*...(tears) A warm feeling inside and an inner smile as I remember 'that time' (more tears).

I feel softer, refreshed, less heavy, less middle-aged as I put this example in the paper.

This is 'focusing on the fly.' I have called it 'mini-focusing' (Friedman 1989). Notice that I do not guide myself through the eight steps. There is nothing sacrosanct about the eight steps. I start right where the 'feltness' is: a heavy feeling in my gut and arms. I follow the felt sense and my visual memories where they take me—to that time in my forties. I cry. The content and the feeling of the issue both change. I allow my nostalgia to be there. I feel lightened.[6]

I go back to the writing.

◆

In the previous examples we have seen more and less practiced focusers working on themselves, sometimes with a guide, sometimes by themselves.

Now I want to turn to five examples of focusing in therapy.

It is not easy to focus alone. **This is worth emphasizing.** Newcomers who try it alone are often disappointed and give up. Like meditation, one often needs a guide. The guide may or may not be a psychotherapist. Credentials and profession count less than a certain quality of the person, training in focusing, and psychological acumen. I focus best with a guide who is empathic, unobtrusive, spontaneously liking of me, unhurried, clear, and knowledgeable of the focusing process. A person who has these qualities and is also a therapist is a real find. There aren't enough such people.

John Welwood is a therapist who uses focusing in his work with clients. In this example he emphasizes what he calls the "unfolding" quality of focusing. New meanings unfold as the client focuses on an experiencing that is always denser, more highly textured, richer than he or she explicitly knows. The presenting problems take a dramatic turn in his or her surface mind. Focusing gets to the heart of the matter:

> A client comes in feeling miserable and depressed. He knows his feelings have to do with his wife, but he does not know what to do about them. At first he talks about his feelings toward his wife and hers toward him, his blame of her and his guilt about that, and so on. But his words are rather lifeless. He is talking "off the top of his head," without any deep inward reference [i.e., focusing] going on. As the therapist, I guide him to find his felt sense of his situation underneath all his thoughts and emotional upheaval. How does he feel it in his body? I let him feel around inside awhile without saying much about it. I next ask him what kind of feeling quality it has (such as shaky, fearful, jumpy, tense, or viselike). "It's a heavy feeling in my stomach," he responds. Now that he is in touch with this heaviness directly, he can begin to inquire into it and unfold its meanings, as presently felt, rather than as he might usually think about them. Such inner questioning is like holding up a frame to this global heaviness, or like shining a flashlight into the darkness. The frame in this case is a question from me: "What is so heavy about this for you?" Again he returns to his felt sense, and we wait for something more specific to unfold.
>
> "It's anger, just sitting in my gut," he now says, "and weighing me down, eating me out from the inside." His

words start to gain vigor and intensity. As he feels around in the anger he has now articulated, the next direction appears: "But even more than angry, I feel terribly disappointed in her. She isn't like her old self." Pause. We are now on the edge of something new. "But I'm also disappointed in myself. Things used to be so good between us, and now we don't even listen to each other." He sighs deeply at this point, as he is getting close to the core of his present feeling. I can tell by his shaky tone of voice that he is close to opening up something larger and more significant. He is no longer talking about his felt sense; he is talking **from** it. His next statement really cracks it open: "And, you know, I'm just now realizing that I haven't let her know how much I care about her in a long time. That's what's so heavy, I've locked up my love and sat on it for months now. I don't know how she even puts up with me." Something in his body is now releasing—he breathes more deeply and looks as though blood were returning to him. He is now in a quite different place from when he first walked in half an hour ago. Each step of unfolding—heavy, angry, disappointed, but particularly this last one—provides what Gendlin calls a felt shift, which forms the basis of genuine therapeutic change (Wellwood 1982, 95-96).

Obviously, something now needs to happen to this man's locked up love. This focusing has not solved that problem. Further focusing rounds—or other experiential interventions—are now called for.

Welwood writes that any life problem usually "has many different strands, but one central tangle (sometimes two or three); many different angles and edges, but one central crux; many irritating aspects, but one central 'rub.' Focusing is not so much concerned with all the twists and turns, ins and outs of a problem or situation so much as its central core"(p. 99). His client's "central core" issue was his locked up love, an issue that pervaded his life. The steps of focusing wended their way to this core issue, as they would have had he started with some other related surface manifestation of the basic issue.

Here is an example from my own work as a therapist. The example illustrates the use of focusing to identify on a felt level a basic syndrome, a broad attitude, a large issue that underpins several specific problems. When the client is focusing at the level of the holistic attitude, he or she is working on each of the related problems at once. This is more economical and effective than taking one troublesome area at a time. "People change," wrote Angyal, "in their roots, not their branches"(p. 205). Focusing gets to the roots.

The client is a 45-year-old former teacher about to go into business for himself. He has had a year of focusing therapy. His eyes are closed. He has put a hefty stack of troubles on the bench and picked one to work on—starting his business. I ask him to attend to the feel of the whole of it:

C: I feel some sort of calm yet urgent and anxious "wanting-to-have-this-done" feeling.

T: A "wanting-to-have-this-done" feeling?
       (Client nods yes and sighs.)

T: (slowly) Let words, images or memories come from that feeling.

C: (After 30 seconds of self-attending) I see myself at the start of a class…ah, ha! It is the same feeling that I have whenever I start a class. (Client wrinkles his brow, like that isn't quite right.) No, it's more like whenever I start a new class. I feel a deeper calm now. I just got the sentence, "Will I be able to do it?" (Client chuckles) Oh yeah, that's the same feeling I often have before I go to bed with a woman for the first time. (Client is quiet again. Next, he tells me what is happening in his body process.) I feel alive and breathing…on the track.

T: (gently) Ask the place where you feel it all—"What's the crux of this?" "What is the main thing about it?"
       A minute passes. I sit and wait. My mind is empty. My attention is focused on him.

C: I'm quiet, listening closely to myself...I want to try out a few possible sentences that feel close to right. "Will I succeed?" (Client shakes his head no.) "Am I Ok?" (He shakes his head. Again, apparently, this is not it. I sit calmly, not rushing in.) Ah..."Can I sustain it?" (Client is quiet. No head nodding. He has been "hearing" these sentences emerge from the felt sense and then checking them against the felt sense.)
        Not quite right, but close. More sentences are coming..."Do I have the persistence? Can I overcome the obstacles?" None feels exactly right, but all feel near the core.

T: (softly, taking my cue from his words) Ask it, "**What's the core of this?**" (My client's response tells me I am on target.)

C: As you said that I felt energy swirling in me. And the sentence, "I'm not sure that I'm enough" came to me. "I'm not sure that I'm enough." (He says it over to check that just **this** is the right sentence, the **name** for the syndrome.) When I said that over I got very still and then really quickly other instances flashed by...the first appointment with a new customer...the way I feel when I wake up in the morning...the way I feel each time before focusing. This feeling about myself holds me back in a lot of ways.

We are now in the phase of focusing Gendlin calls "global application": "The individual is flooded by many different associations, memories, situations, and circumstances, all in relation to the [same] felt referent" (Gendlin 1964). I let the client go on citing instances and then, when the wave subsides, remind him of the key sentence, "I'm not sure that I'm enough." I invite him to begin another round of this feeling process by asking again, "What's the **whole** feel of that?"

Focusing can be very useful when a decision seems to need to be made. Here is another therapy excerpt:

In this next brief example a lot of work has already been done. I have listened to him talk for several weeks about the two women in his life. Mostly, I have reflected back his feelings, asked questions, and disclosed some of my own struggles with the same issue. He has been getting closer and closer to what it is all really about. This is from my notes in my fourteenth session with him:

C: I really want to get to the crux of this issue.
T: So let yourself feel it…really feel the struggle….Can you feel it? (invitation to focus)
C: Uh-huh.
T: Now, ask the feeling—what's the crux of it?

After about a minute, to his utter surprise, he gets a vivid memory of the Vito Antefermo-Alan Minter middleweight championship fight which he had seen the week before. "What relevance does that have?" he asks. I encourage him not to discard it, but to swim around in the image for awhile. Pieces begin to come to him: The fight was very close. The fight was between a boxer and a slugger. *He* couldn't decide who had won. An image of the Marvin Hagler/Vito Antifermo fight now comes to him. (By the way, he is Italian by birth.) That one was called a draw even though he was sure Hagler had won. He chuckles.

We talk. All these magnifications of aspects of the focusing image when empathetically entered reveal important truths about the relationship issue—as does the fact that it is seen as a boxing match! They crystallize perfectly what he had only vaguely and fuzzily sensed as the trouble. At the end of the focusing he feels calm and knows he isn't ready to decide. It is a draw.

Here is yet another example of my using focusing in therapy. An experienced focusing client came into his session newly in love. He spent three-quarters of this session on this very good feeling. He focused on it.

Why? Why would one use a focusing therapy session to focus on a good feeling?

Because therapy is not just about pathology. It is about what is right as well as what is wrong. Angyal notes that "what is right"—what he calls "the healthy system"—gets too short shrift in most therapy.

Therapy needs to demolish the neurotic system and reconstruct the healthy system (Angyal 1965). In this session, I am primarily strengthening the healthy system. Gendlin warns therapists not to be too "pathology oriented." He reminds us "a person is a who, not a what." The "life-forward direction," as Gendlin calls it, needs therapists' abiding attention (1996, chap. 20).

One can learn from good feelings as well as bad. Positive Psychology is now reminding us of this. Focusing does not need the reminder. Focusing is not just remedial. It can be transcendental. It is useful for growth wherever the person happens to be at the moment. Focusing is good both for fixing troubled places inside and for experiencing self-transformation.

In the following example, from his good-feeling place an edge emerges that tells the client something new, something not previously clear about himself and his love. The example shows once again how one's experience always has a "more than what one already knows" quality to it. The example also shows the spontaneous occurrence of other inner processes in the context of focusing. I will note their occurrence in bold face and will comment upon them after.

He comes in, sits down, removes his glasses and shoes, closes his eyes, and begins focusing. He feels a fluttering behind his eyes. His arms want to move. His torso feels spacious, clear. (This is the felt sense.) I ask him for a word, phrase, image, sound or gesture that fits the felt sense.

"Inspired. I feel inspired."

He says the sentence back to himself. "Inspired...I feel inspired". He says that the-thing-in-his-arms has stopped happening. His arms feel lighter and relaxed. The whole of him now feels still. (This is a felt shift.)

He checks the sentence again: "Inspired...I feel inspired." The second check deepens the process. His shoulders want to fall a little. He wants to slow down. There is, he reports, "**A swirling of energy right behind my eyes.**" His attention now is being pulled toward his chest area.

He does not want to put things on the bench. He wants to stay where he is. He asks his chest area, "What is the crux of this 'inspired'?"

He reports an image of a woman and her son. He asks for the whole feel of this image. He gets a faint smile on his lips. His breathing has deepened. He reports feeling warm all over.

"Is there a handle for this new felt sense?" I ask. He says he sees the woman embrace him. His body tingles all over. Inside him he hears the sentence, "I'm in love."

I ask him to check that. He says, "Yeah…I sure am!" His shoulders relax still more. The tingling stops. There is a feeling of "rightness of fit" between the handle and the felt sense. He wants the felt sense to tell him more. I say, "Let's just tap it and see what it sends us." He sees his daughter and the woman's son. They are sitting side-by-side. He feels tears just behind his eyes. "What's that?" he asks himself aloud.

His head jerks suddenly from left to right and back again. A memory from fifteen years ago has popped into his process. He sees himself in his bedroom crying about leaving his little brother. He is going away for a year. Now, the little brother joins the image of his daughter and the woman's son and **the three of them are dancing together**. The image is now a moving picture. He feels "a pleasant kind of teary."

"What kind of 'pleasant kind of teary' is it?"

He says aloud the sentence, "It is a fatherly-kind-of-love," and with that the tears are released. He sits and cries and sobs.

After a few minutes the tears stop and he reports feeling calm inside. An image of his father starts to appear. He is not ready for this next step. So he underlines the phrase "fatherly-kind-of-love" and "something-about-me-and-my-father" as the furthest place he has gone to in this session. About forty minutes have gone by. He puts his glasses and his shoes back on, pays me, and leaves.

Notice in this example the number of felt senses and shifts. What Gendlin calls a self-propelling feeling process has occurred. It has also opened up a slightly altered state of consciousness indicated by the fluttering behind the eyes, the sudden head swivel, and the moment when the image starts to move on its own. In my experience if you see the focuser's eyelids fluttering that is always a good sign. Something is happening. What has happened here is that he has learned some *new information* about his feeling ("fatherly-kind-of-love") and he has released deep *feeling* ("the tears were released").

Notice that in these examples from therapy how little interpreting is being done by the therapist. The therapist does not supply intellectual answers or interpretations. He or she guides a process that facilitates the client's finding—unfolding—his/her own answers. The therapist does not do violence to the client's process.

Notice also the *attitude* that the client takes towards his own experiencing process. As we have seen previously, teaching the focusing method includes teaching a focusing attitude: a reverence for bodily felt experiencing. The client is invited to befriend his or her felt sense of the particular issue being worked on. The message is: welcome it; acknowledge it; open to it; embrace it; let it speak to you; listen to it— the 'it' being the body's current message about the issue. Of course, one would not say all these words but would find the words that best express to this particular focuser the focusing attitude.

◆

At this point I was originally ready to end this essay. Suddenly, a skeptic appeared. The skeptic has read the essay so far. Now he insists on butting in. He has questions. He wants answers. (I have borrowed the skeptic from Dan Wile's excellent book, AFTER THE HONEY-MOON (1988)):

Skeptic: Does focusing always proceed so smoothly as in your examples?

Me: No. See Gendlin's book, FOCUSING for tips on troubleshooting where focusing breaks down.

Skeptic: Is there always such a radical shift in content?

Me: No. I have picked some especially juicy examples.

Skeptic: Does focusing always work?

Me: No. Nothing in psychology always works.

Skeptic: So when are you going to show some less-than-perfect-and-successful focusing?

Me: How about right now?

I am sorry to say that this last example comes from my own practice.

I am happy to say that it comes from 1977 when I was a novice therapist who had just 'learned' (i.e., been exposed to) focusing three years before.

The client is my first client on a day when I am not in such great emotional shape myself.

Notice the clunky way that I introduce focusing into the session. Notice the surface level on which the excerpt stays. Especially notice the absence of sufficient listening responses. I will comment in parentheses on my mistakes and indicate what I wish I had done or said.

C: I'm not sure what to talk about today.
T: So, let's try something new. (I am so eager to introduce focusing that I jump in without even checking that it is Ok with him.) The first thing is to just close your eyes and get comfortable. Take a few deep breaths. Take your time and then signal me when you're ready to go on. (pause) Ok, now just ask yourself inside, how am I right now? Don't answer, but turning your attention like a searchlight to your inside feeling place just greet whatever you find there. How am I inside right now? (long pause) Now, imagine that you're sitting on a park bench…(Again, I am forcing focusing on him. I do not inquire what is happening in the silence or ask him if he wants more time where he is. I am like a runaway focusing locomotive that is going to get its passenger to focus.)…and you're going to stack next to you everything that's in the way between you and feeling all fine right now. So, just say, what is in the way between me and feeling all fine right now? And as each thing comes, just imagine it coming out of you and stacking it a little bit of distance from you. Don't go into any one thing. Just stack.
C: Books.
T: Ah, yes, put them over there.

C: Paper, pencils, tapes.

T: Um, mechanical things. (Why don't I just repeat his list? Why do I have to provide a concept in which to sum them up? Does that influence his next comment?)

C: Mechanicals, drawing boards.

T: Don't go into it, just stack it over there and ask, other than that, am I all Ok? And just wait.

C: (pause) Bank books, income tax, (pause)…

T: Just gently, to yourself, except for this, I'm all Ok, right? (I do not say the things back to him. I wish I had.)

C: Feeling a warm tingle just on the inside of my skin. (pause)

T: (I miss the fact that the warm tingle is the first reference to his body that he has made!) The warm tingle isn't part of the stack. The warm tingle is the result of putting the stack out there, Ok? (pause) Do you want to stay with the warm tingle or—?

C: It changed.

T: It changed.

C: For a moment I dissolved.

T: Um. (I have no idea what he means here.)

C: I could feel the air flowing through me. Now my body is back.

(This may be the most important thing that has happened so far. But it is not part of my mind-set, not part of my "teaching focusing." I should have said, "For a moment you dissolved…and now your body is back." Instead, I let this piece go and stick to the script. I sacrifice the person to the script.)

T: See now whether you want to move toward that stack and feel yourself magnetically pulled toward that one thing in the stack that most needs your attention, the one thing you want to work on. See if you can let it pick you.

C: The drawing board.

T: So take the drawing board and ask, what's the whole feel of that, and that will be the drawing board and all it represents.

Just say, what does the whole of that thing feel like to me? Give your body a nice thirty seconds to get the feel of that thing.

C: (pause) Smooth surface, repetitive motion, glare, sometimes I feel like I can't see. The edge of the board presses into my chest…

T: These are sensations or things about it. Take the issue that the drawing board represents. Is it work or art or I don't know what it is but take whatever it is for you. Say, what does the whole of that feel like for me?

C: I feel tied to it.

(I seem insistent on summing up his details in my concepts. 'Sensations' is my word, not his: I could have repeated his words ["smooth surface, repetitive motions"] or I could have said—"and what is the whole feel of the edge of the board pressing into your chest?")

T: So let's ask it some questions…

(This is bad focusing teaching. "I feel tied to it" is a direct statement of how he experiences the drawing board issue. I should have said slowly and with emphasis "So you *feel tied to It*" and then waited to see where he goes with this. Instead, the script again…and a missed opportunity.)

The session went nowhere. The best that can be said for it is I brought it to supervision and learned some of the points in the parentheses above. The example illustrates that the teaching of focusing in therapy has to be done with sensitivity to the client's process and the interaction of therapist and client (Gendlin 1996).

How do I teach focusing? Gendlin prefers that to learn focusing the person go to a workshop and not have it taught as part of therapy. I do not entirely agree. Sometimes a person comes to me ostensibly to learn focusing but really to get focusing-oriented therapy. So, I lead the person through a round of focusing using the instructions sheet that I have come up with. I may do this over and over for a few sessions and then usually the therapy takes off in various directions.

♦

In sum, focusing can be done either in rounds or in mini-focusings. It can be used both for self-help and in therapy. It is a new addition to the healing process.

A guide leads a focuser. In a whole round, focusing proceeds in steps. The focuser makes contact with a felt sense. As it is befriended and accurately symbolized, the felt sense shifts. Open-ended questions asked of it bring further insights and further felt shifts.

Focusing is about felt senses, a befriending attitude, *accurate symbolization, and felt shifts*. Finding the felt sense is crucial to it. But that is not the whole story. It is a Rogerian-like way to listen to one's own bodily sensed intuitive wisdom. It is a non-interfering way of being with one's own process. It is a friendly allowing-new-stuff-to-come way of sensing into one's inner flow of experiencing.[2]

Honor the felt sense. It has intentionality and directionality. It wants a next step to happen. For the felt shift to occur the felt sense needs to be approached with an unhurried curiosity and receptivity. One does not try to make a felt shift happen. One simply treats the felt sense "nice."

Experiential focusing is a discipline. It is a skill that can be learned. It is a practice. When mastered it makes accessible to a person the intuitive resources that *we all* have inside. It provides the experience that the song lyric proclaims:

> It's in every one of us
> to be wise,
> Find your heart,
> Open up both your eyes
> We can all know everything
> without ever knowing why.
> It's in every one of us—
> By and by.

Five

Listening

Vasudeva listened with great attention. It was one of the ferry-man's greatest virtues that, like few people, he knew how to listen...the speaker felt that Vasudeva took in every word, quietly, expectantly, that he missed nothing...He did not await anything with impatience and gave neither praise nor blame—he only listened...Siddhartha felt how wonderful it was to have such a listener who could be absorbed in another's life.

—Herman Hesse, *Siddhartha.*

Therapists listen. Many of us listen well. Some of us—including myself—do not always listen as well as we think we do. There is a special form of listening—experiential listening—that can help us all be more effective listeners.

Experiential listening is an empathetic, supportive, non-interfering way of saying back to a person the felt essence of his or her message and checking with the person to make sure it has been said back correctly.

Experiential listening helps people clarify and articulate their inner processes, explore issues, get past stuck places, and carry their experiencing forward. It is useful both for non-professional help and professional therapy. *Listening helps people toward their felt senses.*

Put simply: The person being listened to says something. The listener takes the person's whole expression inside, listens to its resonance, and then says back words that point towards the felt sense that has been communicated. Then, the listener checks with the listenee: Did I get that right? If yes, the listenee goes on to whatever he or she has next to say. If not, the listenee corrects the listener, who then tries again to say it just right.

The entire process—"saying back" and "checking in"—is experiential listening.

To illustrate: Consider the following listening I did with a very practiced 45-year-old male client. In parentheses I point out the felt sense and felt shift as they occur.

C: (Matter-of-factly) Let me state the problem as I see it. I have a raging need for autonomy, coming from my mother's having been too close to me. And I have difficulty asserting that need with women…for fear of displeasing them.

T: Let me see if I get that.

C: Ok.

T: (More slowly than C has been speaking) You sense in yourself a need for autonomy, a need that is like a fire, raging out of control.

C: (Interrupting) Yes, but not out of control.

T: (Correcting himself) The need for autonomy is not out of control.

C: Right.

T: (Continuing, slowly) And you sense that that need—stemming from mother having been too close to you—is blocked by an equal or stronger need—coming from the same source—to please or at least not displease women…

C: (Quickly) Yes, exactly…(Pause) When I hear that back, I feel sad and slumped inside. (This is the felt sense.)

T: Sad and slumped come from hearing it back.

C: (More slowly now) Yes…it feels heavy…a heavy burden to carry around.

T: The whole issue feels heavy to you…

C: Right.

T: As if, like some heavy weight you carry inside?

C: (After some consideration) On me…on my chest.

T: You feel as if it sits on you, on your chest.

C: No. Sitting in me, not on me…Pushing down from inside.

T: It feels like a heavy weight inside your chest depressing you.

C: (Quickly) Yes. The image is of a black square.

T: A black square sits in your chest pressing down deep.

C: I sense anger there.

T: The square has anger?

C: No, *underneath* it.

T: Oh…*beneath* the sad and slumped, *anger* lives.

C: (Voice picks up speed and expression from here on) Yes, exactly. When you said that…it moved! I feel it now in my jaw…I'm pissed. Pissed! (This is the felt shift.)

T: The rage beneath the slumped has risen.

C: It's spreading through my body. Wow. Through my arms, legs. My head wants to shake from side to side. I hear the words, "Let me be." "Leave me alone." "Let me be." (felt shift)

T: (With expression rising to match C's) Your whole being is angry!

C: No—*enraged*.

T: *Enraged*!

C: Yes!

T: And just wants to be left alone, let be…

C: The words come in a torrent now…

T: Something has been heard and released in you.

C: (Tears flow) Yes. (Another felt shift.)

T: Like the rivers raging after a thaw…

C: Yes, (Cries) thank you.

As the example shows, listening is a close and careful being with whatever is "inside" a person ("Beneath the sad and slumped, anger lives"), letting oneself be corrected ("No. Sitting in me, not on me"), and thus allowing the "inside" to shift ("The words come in a torrent now…"). Listening is a way of helping a person contact a *felt sense*, a way of keeping a *felt sense* company, and a way of saying it back in such a way that one's words have an *experiential effect*; they permit a *felt shift* to happen (Gendlin 1981).

Listening is useful both in therapy and in non-professional helping (e.g., between friends, spouses, parents and children). Receiving good listening is a powerful, effective, and, for most people, unusual experience. People seldom get to hear back what it is they are groping to express. It is a rare treat to be listened to by someone such as Siddhartha's ferryman who wants you to have the experience of really feeling understood. Everyone deserves the experience of really being listened to. If you have not had it, you don't know what you are missing!

◆

Experiential listening is an offspring of the union between Carl Rogers' "reflection of feeling" therapeutic response and Eugene Gendlin's "experiential method." It can be called "an experiential reformulation of active listening." It deserves to be recognized as one of the latest steps in the evolution of client-centered therapy into the person-centered approach (Levant & Shlein 1984).

"Saying back" is the quintessential helping response in the client-centered tradition of therapy. It has been called variously "reflection of feelings," "clarification of feelings" (Snyder 1947), "active listening" (Gordon 1970) and, simply, "listening" (Gendlin 1981).

Carl Rogers describes its origin:

> Very early in my work as a therapist I discovered that simply listening to my client very attentively [and saying nothing] was an important way of being helpful. So when I was in doubt as to what I should do, in some active way, I listened. It seemed surprising to me that such a passive kind of interaction could be so useful.
>
> A little later a social worker, who had a background of Rankian training, helped me to learn that the most effective approach was to listen for the feelings, the emotions whose patterns could be discerned through the client's words. I believe

she was the one who suggested that the best response was to 'reflect' these feelings back to the client..." (Rogers 1980, 137).

Rogers was a remarkable listener.[1] An excellent sample of his listening style is this excerpt from his work with "Mrs. Oak." In her thirty-first therapy session Mrs. Oak is trying to describe a feeling as it wells up in her:

C: I have the feeling it isn't guilt (Pause. She weeps.) Of course, I mean, I can't verbalize it yet. (Then with a rush of emotion) it's just being terribly hurt!

Rogers: M-hm. It isn't guilt except in the sense of being very much wounded somehow.

C: (Weeping) It's—you know, often I've been guilty of it myself but in later years when I've heard parents say to their children "stop crying," I've had a feeling, a hurt as though, well, why should they tell them to stop crying? They feel sorry for themselves. I thought that they could let him cry. And—feel sorry for him too, maybe. Well, that's something of the kind of thing I've been experiencing. I mean, now—just right now.

R: That catches a little more the flavor of the feeling that it's almost as if you're really weeping for yourself.

C: Yeah. And again you see there's conflict. Our culture is such that one doesn't indulge in self-pity. But this isn't—I mean, I feel it doesn't quite have that connotation.

R: Sort of think that there is a cultural objection to feeling sorry for yourself. And yet you feel that the feeling you're experiencing isn't quite what the culture objected to either.

C: And then of course, I've come to—to see and to feel that over this—see, I've covered it up. (Weeps) But I've covered it up with so much bitterness, which in turn I had to cover up. (Weeping) That's what I want to get rid of! I almost don't care if I hurt.

R: (Softly, and with an empathetic tenderness toward the hurt she is experiencing) You feel that here at the basis of it as you experience it is a feeling of real tears for yourself. But that you can't show, mustn't show, so that's been covered by bitterness that you don't like, that you'd like to be rid of. You almost feel you'd rather absorb the hurt than to—than to feel the bitterness. (Pause) And what you seem to be saying quite strongly is, I do hurt, and I've tried to cover it up.

C: I didn't know it.

R: Hmm. Like a new discovery really.

C: (Speaking at the same time) I never really did know. But it's—you know, it's almost as though I were looking within myself at all kinds of—nerve endings and bits of things that have been sort of mashed. (Weeping)

R: As though some of the most delicate aspects of you physically almost have been crushed or hurt.

C: Yes. And you know, I do get the feeling, "Oh, you poor thing."

(Pause)

R: Just can't help but feel deeply sorry for the person who is you...

(Rogers 1961, 93).

It would be difficult to overstate Rogers' role in the history of psychotherapy. I put him right up there with Freud. His client-centered listening and the philosophy of relationship in which it is embedded changed the course of counseling and therapy. There is a "before Rogers" and an "after Rogers" psychotherapy.

But Rogers' listening is better than his theory of listening. He did it better than he describes it. There has always been a gap in his theoretical writings about listening. It has been mostly unclear just exactly what a "reflection" is supposed to reflect.

This is where Gendlin and his theory of experiencing[2] come in. Gendlin says:

I came to Rogers' group in Chicago in 1952 from my work in philosophy and my interest in the question: How does raw experience become symbolized? I thought that this happens in psychotherapy. A person struggles with and finds words and expressions for unclear—but lived—experience.

I found that Rogers and his group were not very clear in their own minds just what in the client they were responding to. It was the client's 'message' or 'feelings'

(Gendlin, personal communication).

Gendlin's point is that the words "message" and "feelings" are but an imprecise and sometimes misleading shorthand for "unclear but sensed experience." This is the true referent of the reflection of feelings response. It is the felt sense that is reflected.

The concept of "experiencing" and the experiential method specify the referent of the reflection of feelings response more exactly. As we have seen, Gendlin says that there is an ongoing flow of experiencing in the human being. He refers to this as a bodily felt but conceptually vague flow of felt meanings (Gendlin 1962, 1981). The listening response is an attempt to make contact with and carry forward this experiential flow. It is not enough for the therapist to just say back the client's words. *Words are not feelings*. The listener is trying to point his words at the concrete experiential flow for which the listenee is making symbols (words). The listenee checks the listener's words against this ongoing flow. When the listening response is just right, it has an experiential effect—the flow of experiencing is carried forward.

In his last writing on empathy, Rogers acknowledged his debt to Gendlin and made Gendlin's sometimes abstruse philosophical writing more accessible via clinical example:

An example may clarify both the concept [experiencing] and its relation to empathy. A man in an encounter group has been making vaguely negative statements about his father. The facilitator says, 'It sounds as though you might be angry

at your father.' The man replies, 'No, I don't think so.'
'Possibly dissatisfied with him?' 'Well, yes, perhaps' (said
rather doubtfully). 'Maybe you're disappointed in him.'
Quickly the man responds, 'That's it! I am disappointed that
he's not a strong person. I think I've always been disappointed in him ever since I was a boy.'

   Against what is the man checking these terms for their correctness? Gendlin's view, with which I concur, is that he is
checking them against the ongoing psychophysiological flow
within himself to see if they fit. This flow is a very real thing,
and people are able to use it as a referent. In this case, 'angry'
doesn't match the felt meaning at all; 'dissatisfied' comes
closer, but is not really correct; 'disappointed' matches it
exactly, and encourages a further flow of the experiencing, as
often happens (Rogers 1980, 141).

In other words, listening responses are offered in such a way that
they point the listenee in the direction of checking the response (anger?
dissatisfaction? disappointment!) in a focusing way against his/her
experiential flow.

In sum, client-centered listening was a method developed by Carl
Rogers in response to clinical exigencies. It has produced an abun-
dance of practice and research. It has lacked a grounding in a philosophy of experiencing. Gendlin provides that philosophy. The listener
points his response at the felt sense of the listenee. The listenee checks
that response against his ongoing experiential flow. If it is accurate, the
flow moves forward to a next step. If it is not, the listenee corrects the
listener, who then tries again.

This is experiential listening.

◆

How does one do it?

Using the imprecise language of "feelings," Rogers warns that 'feelings' and 'reflecting' them is a vastly complex process" (1980, 138). To
this I can only add—Amen.[3]

What follows is my attempt to describe how I do listening. I was at first tempted to call this section "How to Listen" but discarded that title for the less grandiose "How I Listen." It is as far as I can tell an exact specification of what I do when I am listening well. Others' descriptions exist (Cornell 1993; Gendlin 1974, 1981; McGuire 1981). The reader is invited to compare and contrast.

- I begin my listening by quieting my mind and turning my full attention towards the person to whom I am listening.

There are two steps: quieting the mind; intending towards the speaker.

First, I note whether my mind needs quieting. I do this usually by practicing the first step of focusing. Before my client arrives I close my eyes. I sit comfortably, breathe, and ask myself, "How am I from the inside right now?" I let my attention come down into my body and, in a friendly way, roam or scan around and see what is there. I ask if there is a word, phrase, or image that matches the feeling inside. About seventy-five percent of the time nowadays I get a word like "clear," "calm," "meditative," "open," "ready." I sit with that feeling for a moment and then go to the waiting room to get my client.

The other twenty-five percent of the time I get that I need to do the "clearing a space" step of focusing. I usually put out on the imaginary bench an inventory of what is in the way for me, what is between me and feeling "ready to listen." Most often there will be one or more recent disturbances and perhaps a chronic nagging place in the way. For example, right now I have a pain in my back, left over anger from this morning, and some weariness inside.

By identifying the trouble spots, giving them a moment's quiet attention, and then promising them I will come back and work on them if need be—they agree to mostly clear. I only listen when I'm mostly clear.

Notice that "mostly". Don't make these guidelines into absolutes. I have done good listening while a background upset was not completely resolved. I have done good listening while images from basketball and soccer games danced in the back of my head. There can be background noise in the receiver while one is listening: There cannot be foreground noise.

When we begin to develop the habit of consciously clearing a space, we start to recognize how unclear we tend to be. Many of us much of the time and all of us some of the time are distracted, scattered, not truly attentive, formulating our next point while the other is speaking, drifting off, preoccupied, anxious, angry, defensive, rebutting, interpreting, judging, etc. We are not truly present. We have internal chatter going on. We are not one-pointed (Schuster 1979). It is amazing what all is going on in our heads. The receiver is partly jammed. There is static. We have anxiety, fear, guilt, worry, anger, self-protection, interfering with good contact.

When any of these are happening for you, get listened to yourself. Get listened to about your own barriers and obstacles to good contact with people in general and with each particular person (client) in your life.

Know what it feels like inside when you are clear. Know what it feels like when you are unclear. Know the difference and ways to get from the one state to the other.

A quiet mind helps one listen. Keep working on quieting your mind.

Getting mostly clear is only the first step. From that same space of clarity I can write articles, make decisions in my life, make love, etc.

- Step two is to bend myself toward the speaker lovingly.

I have emptied my mind. I have become receptive—an open channel. Now I 'turn' towards the speaker. I let my whole body express this "turning towards." I make eye contact. I turn my posture in the direction of the person I am to listen to. I lean a little forward. I look inviting and non-intrusive. My body expresses, "I am here to listen to you."

I take in the whole of the person to whom I am listening.

This is a global or holistic "grokking" of the person. I let my "presence" hear his or her "presence." My whole being is listening to his or her whole being.

She comes in. I see her very clearly. Somehow as she sits down I 'hear' inside me the word 'fear.' She starts talking rather vaguely about her job, her week, her relationship. Her posture is a little laid back; her gaze a little glassy; her words a little vague. The whole effect is very subtle. It is more a vibration I am getting from her than her words. I say back, 'So there is something there about your job, your relationship, and your week, and am I getting that that something is fear?' She is startled for a moment. She hasn't mentioned fear. Tears overtake her and they begin to flow. 'Yes,' she says, 'I didn't know. That is exactly what I am feeling. I'm scared…of it all.'

Gendlin states:

> The therapist must attend not only to the client's words but to how they are said, and to how the client is living right in this moment, in saying this. This means observing the person's face, body, voice, gestures, and taking the person in much more broadly than verbally (Gendlin in Corsini 1974, 338).

Narrowness of listening is avoided by this step. When I fail to attend to this step, I may miss the larger message being lived by the person at this moment.

Sometimes I just do this step naturally. Some days I am very tuned in to this level with people. When I am not, it is good to silently remind myself by asking inside, "What is this person's being expressing right now? What is the background feeling from which he or she is speaking? What is the general feeling I have inside as he or she walks in?"

It is worthwhile to remember that people always speak from within feeling states. There is an implicit richness behind every statement one makes. Not everything is or can be made explicit. Often the person is unaware of this background state.

So, I step back, figuratively speaking, and take in a mural sense of the person, attending to the whole feel of his being. I do this even if I don't make explicit use of the information right away, it is part of tuning into the person being listened to:

I am doing a therapy demonstration for a class. She volunteers. She sits down across from me. I observe her eyes: large, open, clear. I take in her erect posture, her bearing, a certain grace in her manner. I hear inside myself the words: 'She is very open and vulnerable, undefended. Just listen to her words very exactly.' I do. She quickly opens up, goes deep, cries, resolves a problem and feels better.

- I reflect back to the person the whole felt essence of what I 'hear' him or her saying.

I would not say all of this, of course, but the experience inside me might be: "Sitting here and emptying myself, I turn my full loving attention toward you. I take in your posture—sitting on the edge of the chair, 'bug-eyed,' a tic in your cheek, a haltingness in your speech. I hear you say you have a final exam tomorrow and feel unprepared. I say back: "So is there some fear, or worry, or concern in you about the final you don't feel prepared for?"

Let me elaborate upon this "saying back" step:

- For every "unit of meaning" I make words that reflect back to the person my best understanding of what he or she is experiencing.

People need to hear you speak. They need to hear that you got each step. Make a sentence or two for every main point they make, for each thing they are trying to get across…Don't just 'let them talk,' but relate to each thing that they feel…Try to get the crux of it exactly the way they mean it and feel it.

Say back bit by bit what the person tells you. Don't let the person say more than you can take in and say back. Interrupt, say back, and then let the person go on (Gendlin 1981, 119-120).

Reflection ought to be fairly frequent. There is no absolute rule. In learning listening, it is best to do reflections more frequently, As your listening becomes more naturally a part of you, you may want to do it less frequently.

It is important to take in only as much as you can hold before reflecting. This amount will vary with your experience level, memory span, and the way your listenee speaks: Scattered speech is harder to hold than connected speech.

- My reflections point toward the felt sense.

There are three different possibilities concerning the relationship between words and felt sense. Sometimes the listenee's words exactly reflect the felt sense. When this happens, the listener says these words back almost exactly:

C: I feel hurt, wounded, pained inside.

T: Hurt…wounded…pained…

C: Yes. Those words are exactly right. When I said them, they felt right inside and when you repeated them I felt them more strongly and clearly…and now I feel a bit stronger.

T: A bit stronger inside now.

C: Yes…it was really fear.

T: The feeling was really fear.

Notice that this is not how people usually talk. It is more how I would wish they talked. More often, the listenee's words only *hint at, suggest, partially express,* or *approximate* the felt sense. They are around or near it.

When this is so, the listener augments these words by making use of whatever else he is picking up from the listenee's non-verbal expressions and whatever else he may guess about the felt sense:

> It is not enough (in this case) to simply say back the content being said. It is also essential to reflect back any unsaid feelings from the person's tone of voice…her body posture, facial expressions and gestures and your own guesses at what a person in her situation might be feeling.

Reflections of unsaid feelings are...offered...as guesses—the person then can check your guess against her inside feelings and come up with a more accurate word. Guesses needn't be right—the important thing is that they lead the person to look at...her feelings, to ask herself, 'Well, if it's not that, what am I feeling about this?' (McGuire 1981, 56).

In the following example, notice how the therapist makes use of non-verbal cues and her own imagining of the situation described and thus helps the client into the felt sense:

C: (Her voice is shaky, quivery, with long pauses) My mother died when I was seven...My sisters were four and two...I had to take over then...I did the washing...the cleaning...got them dressed and all...Then I walked off to school by myself...and a neighbor lady took care of them.

T: (Softly, slowly, with care) I'm imagining you felt very lonely...and sad that you didn't have her anymore...and burdened that you had your sisters to care for.

C: (Tears start to form in her eyes; her words come faster now) Yes, all of that, and now I see that the worst was how *guilty* I felt about leaving them (cries). I didn't do a good enough job.

T: Oh...Like you had loved your mother very much (C: Yes) and what really hurt was your feeling *guilty*...like, you'd let her down.

C: Yes, exactly. She'd left them to me.

Finally, sometimes the listenee's words ignore or obscure the felt sense. Words and felt sense may be like two trains traveling on parallel and non-intersecting tracks. The listenee may know nothing about words coming from felt senses.

The listener then imagines the felt sense that might be there and points at it. More use is made of the non-verbal and the holistic "grokking" than of the verbal productions:

C: (Sprawls into chair, arms akimbo, like a marionette whose strings are being tugged in several directions at once) Well…there's so much to tell you. My week was…I really have to pay my rent…and there was the thing with Charles, oh Lord (a herky-jerky motion; suddenly he sits bolt upright). What was I saying? Oh yes, work was so…Did I tell you about Dorothy? (maniacal giggle)

T: So…does it feel all jumbled inside? Like confused…and maybe all rushing past like an express train?

C: Next stop Greenwich Village!…Yeah (smile) something like that…How did you know? (Friedman 1982a, 103).

It is important for the listener to recognize where on this continuum a person's verbalization is coming from. "Is this particular word or phrase coming from a felt sense?" The listener needs to develop the kind of sensitivity which can answer that question.

Remember that what the listener is attempting to do is make contact with the experiential flow in the client. When words are coming from this flow, saying them back fairly exactly and with intonation, rhythm, etc. that reflect the client's will help make contact with that flow. Words that don't come from this flow are not treated in the same way as words that do come from this flow.[4] Words and the way they are said are clues to the person's felt process. Some clues are better than others. The good listener comes to know which words best point to the felt sense. Sometimes we call them "Neon-signs" words.

Noting where an expression comes from helps guide one as to whether to say something back exactly or paraphrase it—one of the important decisions to be made in listening. A good rule of thumb is to say back almost exactly those words that either match or come from very close to the felt sense and paraphrase the rest.

Clients often say many words that tell the story of external events and few words that describe the felt sense of these events. This is especially so in the early part of therapy. It is the therapist's task to briefly summarize the story of the external events and then highlight the felt sense words.

For example:

C: My father had some medical tests done yesterday. We drove him to Beth Israel and waited there. They gave him the upper and lower GI series. He had to fast all morning and only had some milk all day. We made arrangements for his room and then hung out watching TV. The tests were all negative. Was I ever relieved!

T: The tests were all negative and you felt relieved.

Similarly, a long account of an unhappy vacation was paraphrased, "The trip was unpleasant, and you were disappointed." A detailed description of an argument between two brothers became, "You two fought and it makes you sad and angry."

The same principle applies when the felt sense is not so clearly articulated. The therapist pays special attention here. By pointing his or her reflection at the unclear felt sense, the therapist helps the client grapple with it and become more clear:

C: We went to see The Purple Rose of Cairo. I felt something funny between us during the show. I couldn't really identify it. Afterwards, we had a bit to eat. When I took her home I kissed her goodnight. It was sort of a nice evening, I think.

T: You think you had a nice evening…(more slowly) and there was that something funny you felt during the show…something you felt there.

C: It was like we were and weren't together. I can't explain it…I felt confused by her…and *twisted* by the confusion…I guess it wasn't so great an evening!

T: The main thing there was—*twisted* by the confusion.

Notice that the story line is downplayed and the client's emphasized feeling word (*twisted*) is reflected exactly. As Gendlin says,

> Therapists can paraphrase most of what a client says, but are wise to keep crucially charged words the same. We might paraphrase a long story…But if the client uses the word 'apprehensive,' we would not change it to 'scared' or 'worried' because then the client might lose hold of the connotation that word right now holds. Such a word can be a 'handle' that helps us hold onto a whole suitcase (Gendlin, 1984, 86).

- I vary the way I say things back. Good listening has variety to it. It is creative. It holds the listenee's attention. A steady diet of 'it sounds like you are saying' becomes repetitive, tinny, parrot-like, and artificial. It may put the listenee off.

Therefore, I sometimes affirm my reflection declaratively; sometimes I offer it as a question tentatively.

Sometimes I become the other, as in psychodramtic doubling and say my reflection as though I were he.

Sometimes I do use a 'sounds like you are saying' lead-in.

Sometimes I embellish a reflection by saying the feeling words that had not been said.

Sometimes I pare down and sum up an over-stuffed statement.

Sometimes I rearrange the words in a reflection so as to highlight the felt sense.

Sometimes I add emphasis to sharpen up the feeling tone of a statement.

In the following excerpt I identify in parentheses the several different ways I say things back:

C: I've had enough of going along with other people's cock-eyed opinions!

T: I'm sick and tired of other people's crap! (becoming the other; adding emphasis)

C: Damn right, I've lost myself too often. It makes me so mad!

T: You're pissed about having lost yourself so often. (Paraphrasing and sharpening the language in the feeling words.)

C: More than that—what I've missed in life by being so damn good.

T: Worse than the anger is the missing. (words rearranged)

C: Yeah…I put my own needs on the shelf.

T: You aren't at your center. (Paraphrase; rearranged)

C: It feels awful! I'm wasting my life. I can only live as a hermit. I can't form a relationship. I can only take care of me if there is no one else around. I can't be 'twoed.'

T: Sounds like you are saying that the problem doesn't happen when you're all alone (uh-huh)…but it does keep you from having a relationship (yup)…and since you are really wanting to be 'twoed' (yesiree)…you really feel the need to get this fixed up. ("sounds like" formulation)

C: You got it! Life is with people. I need to learn how to be with people and take care of myself.

T: You are determined to be able to do both. (paraphrase)

C: Yes.

A listening response aims to be evocative. It wants to be vivid. Connotative language (imagery, metaphor, analogy) helps 'spark' the felt sense; it resonates with the ongoing experiencing process.

Therefore, I use imagery, metaphor, and analogy in my listening responses.

Consider these examples:

First, two from Rogers:

C: Well, now I wonder if I've been going around doing that, getting smatterings of things, and not getting hold, not really getting down to things.

T: Maybe you've been getting just *spoonfuls* here and there rather than really *digging in* somewhere rather deeply…(Rogers, in Snyder, 1947, 171).

****

C: I'm gonna take off…I just want to run away and die.
T: I guess as I let that soak in…I guess the image that comes to my mind is sort of a—a wounded animal that wants to crawl away and die (Rogers in Corsini, 1979, 158).

Imagery should be tailored to the vocabulary and interests of the client. Metaphors are personal worlds. *Seldom would I quote baseball to a ballerina.* The image is adapted to the person, not vice versa.

For example, in working with an ardent Zionist I did the following reflection:

C: I want the job at the university. It's special to me. I'm tired of volunteering…and I don't want to teach at the high school level or the state college. I want the university to be my home!
T: "I want Israel. Don't try to sell me Madagascar!"

(Whereas with a baseball enthusiast I might have said, "I'm ready for the Big Leagues. Don't send me back to the minors!")

It helps considerably when therapist and client share a metaphorical realm in which they can communicate vividly and as if in shorthand:

He is a sports nut. So am I. Early on in therapy I get in the habit of sprinkling football, baseball, and basketball images into my reflections: "Sounds like it's the fourth quarter, the score is tied, and you're feeling like the wind is against you"…"You're finally in the batter's box—and there's their ace reliever on the mound." In his focusing, sports images come frequently. One day, for the first time, an ice hockey image appears: "Hey, I just got the winning goal in a Stanley

Cup seventh game!" We note both the winning and the new sport in the image. The next week he reports significant breakthrough activity—in a new realm of life.

Metaphors and analogies related to the client's spheres of interest (sometimes not yet mentioned in therapy) will come spontaneously to the therapist when he or she is especially well tuned in to the client:

C: What's the use? Why bother? Life is a drag and a half.
T: You really feel like giving up!
C: Yeah—really!
T: Sounds like you're at your lowest depths...The underground man.
C: More Dostoevski than Gorki.
T: Raskolnikov?
C: Yes! Exactly! (He brightens up) Murder not suicide!
T: War or peace?
C: War! No question about it! Too much peace at any price.

• After I offer a reflection, I watch and listen to the listenee's reaction, and I am guided by it.

I am explicitly or implicitly asking the listenee to check my reflection against his or her felt sense.

I will discuss three possibilities here: (1) The client doesn't check the reflection against the felt sense. (2) The client checks it, and it is correct. (3) The client checks it, and it is incorrect.

My invitation to the client to check my reflection may be either verbal or non-verbal. If I don't sense that the listenee is doing such checking, I explicitly ask that he or she do so. I sense "not-checking" from the client's continuing to talk rapidly, lack of change of expression on her face, a sense in me that I have not been taken inside, that I have been ignored. When this happens I want to slow up the interaction and explicitly invite her to check my reflection against her felt sense:

C: (Talking rapidly) I'm depressed, down, hassled
T: You're feeling depressed, down, hassled.
C: (Going on over my last word) I don't know what to do—
T: Wait…I'm not sure that you are feeling all that. Would you check?
C: (Confused) What do you mean—check?
T: (Explaining and teaching focusing) Does 'depressed, down, hassled' match what you are feeling in your body?

When I sense that my client is checking my reflection inside, I watch and listen for tell tale signs of whether or not she feels understood. I watch her face, her breathing. Being accurately heard leads to a relaxation. I look to see whether there are signs of that relaxation. Being accurately heard leads to a something new, a sense of further exploration. I listen to whether the next thing said indicates a going further.

Conversely, being inaccurately heard leads to signs of annoyance: a grimace, a squeezing up of the face, a raised eyebrow. Being inaccurately heard leads to the person saying the same thing over again or changing the subject abruptly and staying at a superficial level.

When my client does not feel understood, I drop my previous reflection, let myself be corrected, and try again:

For example:

C: I don't feel understood by Mr. X. He doesn't really see me.
T: You are angry that Mr. X doesn't understand you.
C: No. Not angry. I just don't feel understood.
T: It's not anger. It's being *not understood*. (emphasis)
C: Right. He does what you just did—putting his own interpretation on me. But at least I can correct you!
T: I do it wrong like he does, but at least I can learn.
C: No! At least *I* can correct you!
T: There…I did it again. (Both laugh) The important thing is that *you* can correct me.
C: Right.

- "Checking-in" is as crucial to experiential listening as is "reflecting." Without checking-in, therapy can go off-track:

> She is consulting to the Board of a Corporation. The members can't get along with each other. She intuits a sentence for each to say. It is supposed to sum up each's position. She puts them in dyads and has them say the sentences back and forth to each other. She never has them check the accuracy of her intuition. If she is wrong, there is no correction. They interact around *her* sentence, not *their* own experiencing. Some members leave feeling frustrated, annoyed, not understood. Had she known listening, her intuitive hunches could have been powerfully used; without listening they tended to be wasted or harmful.

Checking-in allows even wrong reflections to be useful, helpful, not destructive. The therapist's 'off-ness' is quickly and easily corrected. The therapist does not lead the client into blind alleys—often, the therapist's blind alleys.

There are two guidelines here: intend to be accurate, and be correctable.

Checking-in takes a burden off the therapist. It is not necessary that your listening always be 'right.' It is necessary that you try to make it 'right,' sometimes succeed, and that you are not ego-attached to your reflections.

Sometimes I demonstrate this last point by saying a reflection in such a way that it *requires* correction.

> There is a lot of feeling in her voice, though few feeling words come through. She is talking about her mother's drug addiction. With long pauses and a sense of heaviness in her throat she says, 'There wasn't…much…I…could do.' Then, she is silent, as she often is. I say, 'I probably won't get all this right, and so you'll have to correct me…but is it like you're

hurt, and disappointed, and, maybe, real mad, or possibly even guilty, that you just couldn't do much for her?'

The form of my reflection shows that it is simply designed to stimulate her to say it the way it was. She responds, "more guilty…less angry…my responsibility."

I often get wrong some part of what a client says to me. I am happy to be corrected. My ego isn't hung-up on being 'right.' I readily drop my reflection and follow the correction.

Being listened to drives this home to me over and over again. A 'wrong' reflection can help me clarify what it was I was trying to say. It can help my self-exploration process. Feeling its 'wrongness' leads me to find words that would be more right. It will only get in my way if you insist on it. If you are willing—nay, eager—to drop it, then I can move on.

I find this one of the most difficult things to teach about listening. Especially to therapists. Many therapists feel that they have to get it right. And many feel that they are always right. I remember telling a therapist that at age four I was cutting a string on my teddy bear, and the knife went into my eye, leading to a traumatic hospitalization and operation. He said, "That was masochism." I stared at him. He was shaking his head affirmatively, agreeing with himself. I said, "How can you be so sure?" He said, dismissively, "I'm sure." His own certainty meant more to him than my hint at doubt. After a few examples of such kinds of intervention on his part, I went elsewhere.

It helps to remember: Listening shows the therapist's *intent* is to understand. Unconditional positive regard is carried by that intent. The energy exchange goes something like this: The client sees the therapist leaning toward him. The client feels hopeful: "Oh boy. It *may* happen here, I *may* be understood." When the therapist is wrong, the client starts to fade, to withdraw, to be deflated. Hope may be dashed. But then the therapist notices the withdrawal. He asks, "Did I get that wrong?" "May I try again?" The client feels hope returning. He may have been too shy, too used to being misunderstood to initiate the correction. But now he responds to the therapist's recognition that he has misunderstood. The client tries again. He tries harder to be understandable in response to the therapist's well-intentioned effort to understand and his willingness to be corrected. Hope returns—so long as listening is successful part of the time and the therapist/listener improves after being corrected.

Hence, the crucial guideline: Don't be attached to your reflection.

In sum, here are my basic directions for listening:

I begin by quieting my own mind and turning my full loving attention towards the person to whom I am listening.

I take in the whole of the person to whom I am listening.

I reflect back to the person the whole felt essence of what I 'hear' him saying.

For every unit of meaning I reflect back to the person my best understanding of what he is experiencing.

My reflections point toward the felt sense.

I vary the way I say things back.

I use imagery, metaphor, and analogy in my listening responses.

After I give a reflection, I watch and listen to the listenee's reaction, and I am guided by it.

I implicitly ask the listenee to check my reflection against his felt sense.

I am correctable. When my client does not feel understood, I drop my previous reflection and try again.

♦

Thus far in this essay I have endeavored to be specific, precise, and analytical about where listening comes from and how I do it.

Now I want to go deeper.

Having engaged your head I ultimately want to speak about the heart.

That is where listening is most appreciated.

Listening helps open the heart.

Let me share with you the occasion for this realization:

> *Listen, listen, listen*
> *To my heart's song.*
> *Listen, listen, listen*
> *To my heart's song.*
> *I will never forget you.*
> *I will never forsake you.*
> *I will never forget you.*
> *I will never forsake you.*
> *Listen, listen, listen*
> *To my heart's song.*

The Opening The Heart Workshop (1996) begins with the group singing these words.[5] I've heard them hundreds of times now. But one day I heard them a little differently. I was working on this essay and I was stuck for a conclusion. I kept hearing the words, "Listen, listen, listen/To my heart's song" over and over. Then my conclusion came to me:

Someplace inside, someplace deep inside, we all want someone to listen to our heart's song.

We want to sing an aria of our pain, a ballad of our love, a medley of our anger, hurt, sadness, and joy.

We want to give voice to what is inside each and every one of us: the particular ways we have been blessed and hurt by life.

We all long to be heard.

But mostly our songs stay inside, shut up.

We move our lips, but we don't sing our songs.

We peek out each from our own cubby hole.

We have walls, masks, moats, gates, fogs, secret chambers, secret police to protect our innermost places.

Why?

Because we have all been hurt by life.

They weren't there. They didn't listen. They were wrapped up in themselves. They told us not to be so sensitive. They showed us not to show our feelings. They told us to act appropriately. They "fixed" things. They yelled at us. They abused us.

Listening is the antidote.

Listening is an invitation to me to sing my song.

Being heard helps undo the hurt.

When I feel listened to I feel better. I feel heard, seen, kept company, understood.

I feel less alone.

I feel supported.

I feel like I have an ally.

I feel the way a team feels when it has a good cheerleading section. I feel more clear.

I feel calm, peaceful, meditative, energized.

My battery has been charged.

The problem may be no different—for now.

But I am different.

My heart is more open.

So remember this about experiential listening: it is a way for one person to really get with and be with another person. The particular specifics of technique are not as important as is this overall effect.

How do I know whether I'm doing it right? I know it by your having the experience of really feeling understood.

Six

Putting Focusing and Listening Together in Therapy

I have given you a broad introduction to focusing and listening. I have taken examples both from therapy and from other parts of life. This has been purposeful. Focusing and listening are not solely therapy interventions. They can be used in other aspects of your life as well. Not everything therapeutic has to go on only in therapy! Too many non-therapeutic things do go on in therapy! As you use these methods more in the various parts of your life, you come closer to living a focusing and listening life. You become a focusing/listening oriented-person.

Now, how does one put focusing and listening together in therapy?

Before answering that question, I want to remind you of something that I said earlier. Namely, that the relationship of therapist and client is of first importance with focusing and listening following. Similarly, as I am about to consider how to put the two methods together, I want to stop and state again that the quality of attention of the therapist, the sincerity of intention that he holds and manifests, his presence, his ability to feel empathetic, real and prizing of the client, his ability to initiate and sustain a therapeutic alliance—all these work on the client even before a single response is given. Do not forget this. Methods and techniques and interventions can be learned. Quality of attention comes more from the therapist's own work on his or her self.

You won't be surprised to hear that there are no rigid rules about how to combine focusing and listening However, after studying many focusing and listening transcripts, I see that there are some patterns of how they go together and that there is an overall aim. Remember that at this point we are only integrating the two main methods of FOT. Their integration with other therapeutic interventions will come in Part Three.

When the therapist begins a session or a segment of a session with listening, the patterns that I see are:

- Listening is used to help a client find an issue, a problem, a feeling, a 'something' that needs to be worked on
- A focusing invitation is used to prompt the client to go deeper.
- What the client says after he focuses is met with a listening response.
- An invitation to focus is tacked on to the end of a listening response.

Each of these bulleted features can be used by itself as well as with the others.

For example, here listening is used to help a client "land"; that is, find what it is that needs his attention today:

C: I'm feeling…some hesitation, some assertiveness, some fear, and something else like…(voice trails off)

T: So, there is some hesitation, some assertiveness, some fear, and a something more that you don't yet have words for.

C: Yes. That is right. When you said it back, the 'fear' is what resonated the most.

T: You want to explore the fear more…

This second example puts bullets one and two together;

C: I'm a little all over the place today…Let's see…there is my grandmother's upcoming visit, my daughter's play, and the thing with my husband and…

T: So, grandmother's upcoming visit, daughter's play, the issue with your husband, and…

C: Funny, when I look inside the thing after the 'and' is what most grabs me. I did not know that…I did not know that was even there…shopping for the holidays.

T: So, shopping for the holidays has the most charge to it?

C: Yes.

T: Can you go see what the whole feel of that 'shopping thing' is for you?

If the client responds in a focusing way then the therapist uses the third bulleted item:

C: (continuing the above, eyes closed) The whole feel of it is…both dreaded and excited…

T: Both dreaded and excited…

In this example all four bulleted items go together:

C: I'm unsure about what to work on today. I have a few possibilities: my relationship situation, my health, and my daughter.

T: There is your relationship situation, your health, and your daughter. (listening)

C: I want to concentrate on my daughter.

T: What is the whole feel, the whole felt sense of your daughter?'(focusing invitation)

C: Awesome….exciting…happy…bouncy…

T: So there is awesome, excited, happy and bouncy (listening). Could you tap into all that? (focusing invitation)

When the client begins the session or the segment of the session with focusing, then the guidelines are the same except the first one is dropped. The client has already landed in his body. The therapist says back the essence of what the client says in his focusing. Then, the therapist adds another focusing question onto the end of the listening response.

In the following example we follow a therapist and client through a number of interactions that illustrate the use of focusing and listening:

The client is in a training group. He closes his eyes and goes inside.

C: I am standing on the edge of a deep black hole.

T: Right there on the edge of a deep black hole. Can you stay right there on the edge of it? (focusing invitation)

C: Yeah...I'm curious, one part of me is...and there is another part that wants to have something to hold onto.

T: There is a curious part...and another part...and is that part fearful?

C: No.

T: What would that part like to hold onto?

C: It wants a railing around the hole and a rope to hold onto.

T: So...a railing around the hole and a rope to hold onto. Could you choose? (clumsy question).

C: No, I need both.

T: So, there you are with a railing around the hole, you near the railing, and also a rope holding you back. Is that right?

C: Yes.

T: Can you go see what wants to happen next?

C: There is a little child in free fall down the hole, but it isn't scared.

T: A little child in free fall and it isn't scared.

C: And a section of the railing is crumbling.

T: So, there is a child in free fall who isn't scared and a place where the railing is crumbling and you still have that rope around you...

C: Yes.

T: Can you sense what all of that is? (focusing invitation)

C: There is a bright neon sign on the wall and it says 'Life'…It is insecure; it looks dangerous; it isn't all that dangerous.

T: Oh, it is a picture of life itself, a painting called 'Life'

C: It's not a painting.

T: I take that back (both laugh). It is not a painting. It is Life itself.

C: Yeah. And I still have the rope around me. Life is not as dangerous as it appears. The baby won't hit bottom.

T: The message seems to be that life is not as dangerous as it appears—

C: It is more secure.

T: more secure…We need to stop in a moment. Is there any last thing—

C: I want to sit back against the wall (of the room) in a chair that has secure arms, and watch the scene from not so close to the hole. (He so relocates his chair. End of session)

Aside from these patterns the main thing that I see is that focusing and listening are used by the therapist to stay close to the moment-to-moment experiencing in the client. How this is done probably varies from therapist to therapist and client to client. Again, no rules. But, an overall aim is to keep the client friendly company.

♦

I want to make a comparison here. I have been in two analytically-oriented therapies. How do they differ from Gendlinian therapy? In each of the analytically-oriented therapies (one of which was quite productive) I may have talked for anywhere between ten minutes to a half hour before the therapist said anything. What the therapist said then was usually an interpretation or a question, or, towards the end of the session, a summing-up and weaving together of the themes from the session. Usually, I had the feeling of being somewhat understood. A lot was left out and never got a response. I never had the feeling of my moment-to-moment experiencing having been closely followed and kept company. It was not a moment-to-moment kind of thing. That is what I believe is unique to focusing-oriented therapy.

Yet, a really good dynamically oriented therapist could sometimes bring together things that I had said five sessions before and relate them to what I was saying now in quite an impressive way. This therapist took copious notes in each session but quite unobtrusively. I let her know how my own way of doing therapy differed form hers and how I disagreed with some of her "rules and regulations" for doing therapy. I felt well heard there. She simply acknowledged our differences and kept on as was right for her. I did feel understood, but I did not hear my words back moment-to-moment.

So, just as there is more than one way to skin a cat, as the saying goes, there is more than one way of doing good therapy.

Back to our good way.

Look at another sample of Gendlin using focusing and listening in therapy. Notice how closely he sticks to the client's words. This is how I experienced him also and although I do not stay quite as close—I mean, line for line—my tendency is in that direction.

The first excerpt is from the very beginning of an early session:

C: I've been looking forward to coming, much more than I did the other times. I've had a crummy week. My job is really bad, and I'm tired of my house, everything seems flat like I'm just watching. I'm not in it. And I know it's me.

T: So everything seems flat and you're not involved in it, just watching. But you know it isn't the job and so on, it's you.

C: Well, the job really is bad, what they're doing in that place isn't right. But other times I'd be able to do something with it, I know.

T: So it's true what you feel about them, but also the way you're being inside you is not ok.

Gendlin rearranges her words so that the reference to her inside feeling place is the last thing she hears.

From later in the same session:

C: I have lots of energy there, but it's tied up.
T: You can feel your energy right there, but it's tied up.
C: Yes.
T: Can you sense what is tying it up? (invitation to focus)
C: It's like a heavy wall in front of it. It's behind that.
T: You can feel a heavy wall.

(Long silence)

C: It's a whole part of me that I keep in.
T: Did you say a 'whole' part? (I thought she might have said 'old').
C: Yes, a whole part of me, like when I say it's okay when it's not. The way I hold everything in.

(Long silence)

C: There's a part of me that's dead and a part that isn't.
T: Two parts, one is dead and one, uh—
C: Survived.

(Silence)

C: It wants to scream.
T: The dead part wants to scream and be let out (listening particularly well)
C: To live.

(Long silence)

C: And there's also something vague. I can't get what that is.

Gendlin zeroes in on the vague something.

T: Make a space for that vague thing. You don't know what it is
          yet. There's something vague there, but it isn't clear what it is.

They take a break for a cup of tea as Gendlin feels she has been
working very hard in the session and needs a break. The next excerpt
comes from after the break.

C: Now I'm going back.
T: There was a vague thing and tension.
C: It's like I want to run.
T: Step back just a little step and be next to the wanting to run.

Notice how Gendlin has used a leg-related image (Step back...) to
invite her to focus on the wanting to run.

(Long silence)

C: Someone will be mad at me if I let that part live and that's very
          uncomfortable.
T: If you let that live, someone will be mad at you, and that's hard
          to stand.
C: Yes.

(Long silence)

C: I want to run and never look back and just be free.
T: You want to run, just not look back, go free.

(Silence)

C: Then, that's sad....

Let's stop here although the excerpt goes on (Gendlin 1996, 112-165).

Notice that Gendlin is right there with his client every step of the way. She feels understood on a moment-to-moment basis. This is a good sample of his work relatively early in therapy with a high experiencing client.

Another example comes from my own work. It shows my movement back and forth between focusing and listening. To the extent that I can I will comment upon the decisions I made in this transcript. The transcript starts with more listening and then moves in a later session to more focusing. More listening comes in the earlier sessions. More focusing comes in the later sessions.

Why?

Some clients take better to listening than to focusing (and vice versa.) At some points in therapy clients have a need to talk, to tell their story and have it taken in and responded to.

Other clients (or the same ones) at times have the need to go inside, feel their felt senses and report them. They do not want the interaction the people do who want to be listened to. Two different types of interaction are involved. The therapist builds up a sense of what kind of interaction the client needs at just *this* moment. Notice how my sense of what is needed changes in my work with this client.

The first excerpt is from the third individual session with a man whom I had previously seen eight times in a group. His male lover has just left him. They had made a date to meet on the corner of 45th and Madison Avenue in New York City. The lover didn't show up, and my client never saw him again.

We will follow this client through several sessions. He begins the session tending to deny his feelings:

C: (flatly) In general I feel pretty good…(with more feeling) but I'm more in touch with a…sadness. (For a second he looks sad; then he lifts himself in the chair and out of the sadness) I mean I'm just as happy as ever; everything's going well; that hasn't changed; I'm not in pain (his voice trails off).

T: So, everything is going nicely and you're not in pain...but, you're more in touch with (slight pause, said deliberately) a sadness...(I rearrange his words so as to emphasize the sadness feeling)

C: Yeah. You bet I am...(reflectively) I came to one realization that is hard to talk about...when I do feel sexual (shifts in the chair; starts over) When I *did* get a feeling of sexuality...sometimes it is somebody I even *despise* or is contemptuous of me that I choose.

T: (reflecting the feeling) "I feel uncomfortable saying this to you but I like...no—sometimes I'm *attracted* to someone...either that I *despise* or who is *contemptuous* of me..."

C: Yes. Definitely. (He goes on to feel his way further into his attraction to the other's contempt for him)

The same client, the next session. He talks about how he has helped a fellow worker to go on a diet even though he doesn't really like the person. The description is in monotone. Then:

C: I'm jealous! (Firmly) I don't want him to lose weight. He looks at me as someone liberated, free, and I won't let him know I'm really unhappy. I'm putting on something of an act. I'm *happy* seeing him not making progress...I guess part of it is I feel *I'm* not making all that much progress and so why should I encourage him to jump ahead?

T: So there's a feeling there—*I'm* not making all that much progress—(I highlight the feeling expressed)

C: (cutting me off, more emotionally involved) No, I'm not! I guess *that's* what bothers me. If *I'm* happy and content I don't care what others do

T   (reflecting the feeling that sounds strongest) "Why help him when *I'm* not happy with my own progress! Is that right? (invitation to check-in via focusing)

C: Yes, that's the anger. Why doesn't someone ever encourage *me*?

T: Yeah—where is there someone for me?

C: I'm helping all these people. (with more feeling) It *annoys* the hell out of me…(He goes further into his anger and annoyance with all the people who don't inspire him and I ought to have indicated that I may be one of them.)

Notice that thus far I am mostly doing listening with him.

My listening response is directed at both the *expressed* and the *inchoate* feeling in the welter of words that has just come. It is a gentle lowering of the person into that from which his words have emerged. Listening is helping a person sense and "get into" rather than merely "talk about" feelings. Gendlin describes this as finding the trap door, the deepening response which helps a feeling open. If what is still implicit, pre-conceptual, forming in the client's message, is responded to empathetically, then the person moves forward one step further beyond what he/she has already symbolized.

A third example with the same client captures more of the "trap door" phenomenon. I listen for and reflect the feelings *beneath* the words:

The next interview. He is talking about his ended love affair.

C: I really wanted him. It was like his body was on fire. I went home and rubbed an urn…like a prayer. (He is embarrassed)

T: (gently) You were really hot for him, so hot you prayed he'd come back…Was there a feeling there…I really wanted him…but I didn't…*deserve* him? (tentatively offered guess as to what feeling may be there yet unexpressed.)

C: (sadly) Yes. (tears)

T: (repeating—slowly) I didn't *deserve* him…

C: How could *I* have been so lucky!

T: (expressing the feeling that may be there) I feel so…unworthy…

C: No. More like…grateful to the gods.

T   Oh, so it's not *unworthy* so much as *grateful* for outside forces sending him to you (correcting myself based on what he says)

C: Yes. I couldn't have gotten him on my own...I guess you're right. I don't feel I was worthy of him. He was in another league...I'm an understudy. He was the star of the show. God, I wanted him...Like the shoreline wants the sea.

T   It was like a natural craving, two pieces that needed each other to be complete, to make a whole...maybe like an inferior being needs a superior being to raise him up, to make him more, to fill him?

C: Yes...I felt stronger when he was inside me (tears) I hear Roberta Flack singing, "That's just the way life changes/like the shoreline and the sea..."

T: (finishing the song; I know it well) "Hey...that's no way...to say good-bye..."

C: (deep, heavy sobs)

T: "I yearn for him so..."

C: (nods his head and cries more)

In these three excerpts we see a progression. The client entrusts me with increasingly deeper material. At first he denies feelings. He cuts me off lest I get too close to him. Then, as I carefully empathize, he opens himself up more both to himself and to me.

Where is the focusing? Thus far I have not used it much with him as there has been so much mileage gotten from the listening by itself. Now, I begin to slip in focusing.

In the example below, I italicize the focusing questions.

Same client, next session.

C: I'm feeling tired and heavy and not really pleased with what I'm doing.

T: Hmm. Tired, heavy, and not really pleased. *What's the quality of that whole feeling?*

C: (crinkling up his nose) Sort of blah, flat, unenthusiastic.

T: Blah, flat, unenthusiastic.

C: Yeah.

T: *Can you just tap up against all that?*
C: It's teary and envious. I see my friend Bob's face and I'm jeal-
        ous that he is so inspired.
T: Some tears there for you, for yourself, and envy of him. "He has
        it and I don't!"
C: Yes!
T: Unhappy with you and jealous at his inspiration…*Go see what
        that is.*
C: I feel deprived! It is the same theme again but in new territory.
        No one feeds me! At least, not enough. I don't have enough
        inside and not enough is coming from the outside. He is more
        fortunate than I. (end of excerpt).

I am still doing a lot of listening with my client but now I am adding focusing questions onto the end of my listening responses. That is how I brought focusing in with him.

Finally, let me acknowledge that in this chapter I have concentrated on sessions where focusing and listening and their working together has proceeded without obstacle. In the example with my client, I do miss a couple places where I could have tentatively asked whether I am included among all those people that are not helping him. It would have been better to work that issue (the 'him and me' issue) in there too.

Focusing and listening do not always work this well. Some people, as we have seen in the chapter on focusing, seem practically allergic to focusing.

So do some with listening. I have found such people quite often to have a problem with intimacy. They either feel that their autonomy is being threatened or they are paranoid about why the therapist wants to stay so close by saying back what they have said. (This does not necessarily apply to professionals in the mental health field who may have just had an overdose of Carl Rogers!) Of course with some clients simply explaining what listening is about helps but not with all.

Sometimes the integration of focusing and listening is not as smooth as it is in these examples. People wander off the subject, refuse to land on the airfield runway, make a mid-air connection with some other flight, do not open the trapdoor. Whatever the metaphor, combining focusing and listening is not always as smooth as these examples indicate. But, the therapist's aim is clear: to stay in close connection with what is going on in the client, to follow it along, to keep it company, to help it to move forward.

With the caveat that integrating focusing and listening is not always as easy as our examples indicate, let us move on to consider the integration of focusing and listening with other methods.

Part Three

Beyond Focusing and Listening: Integrating Other Methods

Integration is one of the hallmarks of Focusing-Oriented Therapy. I combine focusing and listening with other kinds of interventions to get a more fully robust Focusing-Oriented Therapy. You can integrate them with whatever you already know. Now, I talk about my own way of combining them with other methods.

Seven

The Integration of Focusing and Listening and Other Verbal Interventions

In what follows I am going to talk about *verbal* and *body-centered* therapies. This is not a perfectly symmetrical dissection of the therapy world. For now it will do.

Verbal therapies are better known than body-centered therapies. By verbal I mean that the therapeutic event is largely a verbal exchange between client and therapist. Usually, the client says more. The therapist says less. There are silences. The therapist does not touch the client. Nor does he or she consciously aim his or her verbalizations at the client's body.

There are many verbal therapies. Cognitive Therapy, Behavioral Therapy, Modern Psychoanalysis, Existential Therapy, Rational Emotive Therapy, Cognitive-Behavioral Therapy, Family Therapy, Couples Therapy, and Reality Therapy are all examples of verbal therapies.

There are also body-centered therapies. I will name some of them in the next chapter. Body-centered therapies involve either the therapist touching the body of the client or aiming his verbal responses at the body of the client. Body-centered therapies include verbal exchanges but verbal therapies do not include body-centered interventions.

In this chapter I am going to take up several kinds of verbalizations that I use in a verbal focusing-oriented therapy and illustrate how they are integrated with focusing and listening. I will start out with verbalizations closest to focusing and listening and expand my range from there. Once again we will visit focusing to get started.

What do I do in a verbal focusing-oriented therapy? What kind of interventions do I make?

• **I do focusing.**

Focusing is basic to my therapeutic work. I know we have already talked a great deal about it. I have something to add about it here.

I am asked often by other therapists how I introduce focusing into my therapy. These therapists have been exposed to focusing. They are intrigued by it. They are unsure as to how to present it to clients. As one said, "It is something new. It seems powerful. How do I bring it into my therapy work?"

There are two main ways that I introduce focusing into therapy. One way is "focusing rounds." I lead a person through the eight steps in which I teach focusing.

The other way is "mini-focusings." I tuck invitations to focus inside other verbal exchanges. This may mean one, two, or three focusing steps embedded in some combination of listening, self-disclosure, asking questions, giving feedback, making interpretations, verbal gestalt experiments, etc. We will see examples of these combinations of responses later in this chapter.

Before we get to them I want to show what a round of focusing can do all by itself.

I do focusing rounds when (a) a person has come to me explicitly for focusing therapy; (b) after I have had a person read FOCUSING; (c) when a client who knows something about focusing comes in with nothing pressing to work on and wants to practice focusing.

I do not do this very often. One out of every fifteen sessions a week may look like the following:

> She comes in, takes off her glasses, closes her eyes, and gets comfortable in the chair. We have contracted for a whole round of focusing as part of the ongoing therapy that she is in with me.

T: Take a few deep breaths…Imagine your attention is like a searchlight…you can turn the searchlight on and shine it down inside your body….Just see what's there…

C: (30 seconds) There's a knot in my stomach…and I want to curl down over it (curls). I want to slump.

T: There's a knot, and you want to slump, to curl over it.

C: Yeah.

T: Should we stay with it for a moment or put things out on the bench?

C: Let's put things on the bench.

T: Ok…Imagine you're sitting on a park bench…you're going to stack, at a comfortable distance from you—down there on the other end of the bench—whatever is between you and feeling all fine right now…Just ask, "What's between me and feeling all fine right now?"

C: (after a minute of silence) There's this trouble with my child.

T: Trouble with your child.

C: Yeah…then there is this new thing with my boss.

T: The new thing with your boss.

C: Yeah…Then there is the whole thing about my job—whew—that's a big one.

T: There's the big one about your job.

C: (quiet for about 30 seconds) There are a few other minor things…my elbow…missing judo class…some trouble—small—with Martin (her husband)…

T: Whew! Let's slow it down…There's the elbow—

C: Yeah.

T: Missing the judo class—

C: Yeah.

T: And the small thing with Martin—

C: Yeah…(perks up) Maybe it isn't so small!

T: Anything else? See if there is anything else that needs to go out on the bench. You are looking there for a feeling of a little more space inside, not quite so jumbled up there….

C: (after a minute). No. I think that is all. Could you say them back to me?

T: (repeats each thing)…Now, first take a moment to feel that there is a "you" separate from all that stuff…(twenty seconds). Then, let yourself feel pulled toward the one thing in the stack that most needs your attention right now…

C: (quickly) Ha! I'm surprised. It's the thing with Martin.

T: Ah, yes. The thing with Martin…Now, hold it in front of you, this thing between you and Martin, picture it, say its name over and over…and give your body time to get the whole feel of it…let the whole feel of it form….

C: (after about a minute) That's the knot, and the wanting to curl over it…I'm afraid I've hurt him and he'll leave.

T: So, it's the knot (yeah)…and it's the wanting to curl over it (yeah), and you're afraid you've hurt him and he'll leave.

C: Yeah…(starts to cry at first a little and then convulsively) I'm afraid he'll do what Faith did (a woman lover who left her).

T: Ah…there it is…you're afraid that it will happen again (yeah)…He'll leave like Faith did…(Yeah. I hand her a tissue.) Does that feel like the crux of it?

C: Yep. That is sure it. (She is sitting up more erectly now, almost with a rueful smile on her face. There has certainly been a shift.)

T: Can we ask it some questions?

C: Sure. Why not?

T: Ask it…(I struggle to come up with what feels like a right question. I'm not sure and so pick a general one)…Ask it—what's wrong?

C: (very quickly) What's wrong is I'm a scaredy cat! Once burnt, twice shy! Every time I get mad at him—boom. Faith redux.

T: (I could repeat this, but she seems to be suddenly on a roll, and I don't want to get in the way. So I move right to a next question) Ask it, what does it need?

C: It needs some courage, damn it. I'm no cowardly lion. (She is laughing by this point)

T: Ask it, what's a good, small step in the right direction?

C: I'm going to go home and tell him—you're not Faith! You're not Faith! That's funny. I feel like a character in the "Crying Game"! Hey, when I said that the knot left…Jesus Christ…I'm tired of being haunted by ghosts…

T: See if there is any other question the felt sense wants to be asked.

C: Yeah. How long does this have to go on?

T: Ask the felt sense—with caring—how long does this have to go on?

C: (slowly) It says—"Till you really get it."

T: Get what?

C: (breaks into sobs) That I didn't cause Faith to go away…(more tears)

T: Yeah…that you weren't responsible for Faith's leaving.

C: Yeah.

T: Yeah…Does that feel like a good stopping place? (There is about five minutes left in the fifty-five minute hour, and she has begun to reach for her glasses.)

C: Oh, yeah, I guess so. Boy, I didn't know that was there. Thanks. (We hug)

Notice: (1) The client is surprised by what she chooses to work on. (2) There is a real felt shift during the session. (3) I mostly pick and choose focusing questions to ask. (4) Often I reflect back what she has said. (5) There is a lot of emotional expression (catharsis) in the session. I never interrupt it. (6) I follow her lead and what I know of her story so as to tailor the focusing round to her needs. (7) I ask whether we have reached a place to stop.

This is fairly representative of what a focusing round looks like. The whole encounter has consumed about thirty minutes. (She was ten minutes late to start.) And we covered a lot of ground in that thirty minutes.

- **I do listening.**

I do not have anything to add to what I have already said about listening but I did just want to remind us that it comes right alongside focusing.

- **I make content-less statements designed to keep a person at a feeling place.**

We therapists have the idea we always have to be doing something. We have to be saying something smart. We have to be devising a brilliant experiment for the client to do. We have to be formulating a right diagnosis that sums up all the material the client has given us. We have to give a brilliant depth interpretation of what the client is really saying.

Sometimes all that is wrong. We have to be doing something, in fact, quite simple: keeping the client company.

I have said that the immediate goal of my sessions is to get a feeling process going and then to stay with it, allowing it to deepen. Some clients most of the time ("externalizers") and most clients some of the time start to touch a feeling and then whoosh off—out of the feeling, on to the next story. I want them to stay where they are when they are "at" or "into" something. I want them to let it register, to resonate with it, to savor it. So, now and then when I sense that they are about to desert their experiencing I will simply underline with a content-less statement that, at this moment, they are in touch with something in themselves, something that deserves our attention. I'll say:

> *That's* heavy.—
> Let's make some space for *that.*—
> You sure have a strong feeling *there.*—
> Wait a minute! Let's take *that* in…—
> *Aha! That's new…Let's be with that…*—
> *Whoa! Tread water there. Let's just hang out with that feeling and listen to it.*

My aim here is to turn what may become simply yet another fleeting moment of experiencing into a meaningful and therapeutic moment when the client hangs out for some time with something inside that is visceral.

- **I make content-less statements designed to bring a client back to a feeling place.**

Despite such efforts clients often flee the feeling, get away from their process. If they move on to another felt place, that is fine. But if they start intellectualizing, externalizing, telling stories, making cocktail conversation, commenting on world history, then I will try to bring them back to that felt edge, the feeling place they had scooted away from. As soon as I get a chance I'll say:

"I'm still sitting with the feeling, 'He won't respect *my* space.' Could you go back and sense the flavor of that?"

"I'm still back where you said, "I'm so *mad* at her!" Could you go back and touch that 'mad'?"

As you see, I often follow "come on back" responses with process furthering focusing instructions.

Let us now look at some other verbal therapist interventions that are a little further away from focusing and listening.

- **I self-disclose.**

In my experience I use self-disclosure more than do many of my colleagues. I do not know why that is. It may have to do with my not having had analytic therapies early on. I never got that "the therapist as mirror" thing. It is clearly outdated. It seems strange to have to make the case for self-disclosure at this time. I would think everybody was more into it.

This is a subject I feel passionately about so let me add the observation that it is striking how many analytically-trained therapists looking back on how they practice differently from the way they were taught, mention self-disclosure (Shay and Wheelis 2000, e.g., 79, 117, 154, 158). My favorite example comes from Sophie Freud, Sigmund's granddaughter:

> A woman in her late forties, of apparent middle-class status, presented me with an 'impossible situation'. Her former husband had chosen to live next door with his new wife.

Every time she stepped out of doors she had to watch the wife work in their garden, or sip lemonade on the porch. It was a constant source of chronic irritation for her. After some discussion, I said I knew exactly how she felt. I had once lived in a situation where my ex-husband with his new partner occupied the flat adjoining mine. While taking my daily bath I could almost hear them making love on the other side of the wall. We both started to laugh, totally and heartily, about the absurdity of life, about our common destinies as women, about shrugging one's shoulders at the inevitable and going on with life. My client stood up, clasped my hand in gratitude and said she could manage from now on (in Shay and Wheelis 102-103).

John Rowan and Michael Jacobs have combined on a book called The Therapist's Use of Self (2002). I don't like that 'use of self' phrase, but the book has quite a lot to say for self-disclosure.

It seems to me that a certain anachronistic homage to the analytic tradition is what basically still stands in the way of therapist self-disclosure.

The Jungians have always on the whole been more available to their patients than the Freudians. Wheelright, a Jungian in San Francisco who spoke at a seminar during my clinical training at Langley Porter Neuropsychiatric Institute has said:

"I don't conceal myself. I frequently use myself as a therapeutic instrument, and I don't try to be anonymous. Often I share my feelings with analysands…" (in Rowan and Jacobs, 64).

He goes on to say that how and when he will share his feelings depends upon his assessment of the analysand's readiness to hear what Wheelright has to say.

Rowan and Jacobs go on to say that "the humanistic tendency is to self-disclose" (p. 63) and then go on to add six pages of examples drawn from several different humanistic schools. After that they do indicate that there is a splintering within the psychoanalytic tradition with some analysts now speaking out in favor of self-disclosure.

I really do wish that more self-disclosure were the norm in the therapeutic way of being today. When a self-disclosure is followed (if necessary) by a listening response in which the therapist checks in with the client as to how the self-disclosing comment was for him or her, then I cannot see self-disclosure being so dangerous for the progress of therapy.

At the same time let me make it clear that I do not disclose everything. When I had to wear a removable splint on my thumb recently, I always took it off while doing therapy. I did not want it to become a subject of conversation.

Similarly, when my wife and I separated I specifically did not tell the couples I was working with who were contemplating separation. They did not need to hear about mine.

People change through direct emotional experience. Clients can have such an experience with a therapist who is *there, present, real, responsive*. My expressions of my experiencing process facilitate mutual, spontaneous, feelingful encounter (Kempler 1981).

I am a very human therapist. I express my feelings when my client is stuck—going nowhere, externalizing, intellectualizing, making small talk, not engaging me and therapy. I do so also when clients are with their feelings, I have feelings related to theirs, and expressing mine will probably move us forward.

Sometimes it doesn't. But so long as I quickly check in with my client after an expression of my feeling, no harm is done. *Checking-in is crucial. This means following-up a self-disclosure with a return to listening.* That way if I'm off the track, we get back on it. And if my client doesn't want to hear from me, he tells me, and I respect his choice.

It is important that I carefully delineate my own feelings, express them as my own, and then wait, patiently and eagerly, for what comes next from the client. I want my clients *present*, wholly engaged in our interaction. I don't want them parceled out, divided, neither here nor there. So it is important that *I* am fully present, responding from *my* center, not drifting off, analyzing, staying aloof. Only then can we meet each other.

I do two different kinds of self-disclosing. I tell things about myself. These are not here-and-now things. They are personal sharings in the way that a good friend may tell another good friend about his life. I do this to make myself more real to the client, to share things we have in common or to emphasize my unique difference from him or to teach something by example. I do this unobtrusively and briefly. I don't hog the session. In a sentence or two I say something about myself that aims to build our relationship. Then I go right back to listening.

The second kind of self-disclosure, the one I will show here, is here-and-now sharings of my present experiencing. An example from the therapy with my abandoned client shows how these brief personal sharings often propel therapy forward:

C: We had made a date for Friday night. It was December 22, 1976. We had been together for seven months. I was waiting on the corner of 45th and Madison. He never showed up. He never called. When I got home there was a note saying he didn't want to see me anymore.

T: How heartless!

C: You sound angry.

T: You're damned right I'm angry! I'm angry for you...and I'm also angry for when something like that happened to me.

C: I wasn't angry...I never told anyone this...(sobs) All night I pretended he was still with me. I made dinner for us. We sat and ate together. I slept next to him...In the morning I admitted he was gone.

Here is another example with a different client:

C: (never shares his feelings with anyone. He comes in looking sad and fearful. He says he wants to share his feelings with me. For my own reasons, unconnected to him, I'm feeling very teary myself. I sigh deeply in response to his saying he wants to share his feelings. Tears come to my eyes. He looks afraid.)

C: I get unfocused when I hear you sigh.

T: And see the tears in my eyes.

C: Yeah.

T: What does it do to you?

C: (looking at the floor) It gets me scared…(pause, he looks up and at me) I don't feel so scared now, but I feel odd. It feels *weird* that you react like that…I guess it's because when I cry I feel weak…and bad

T: When I cry I sometimes feel strong and good. (He starts to weep; I start to weep. Despite weeping, I keep my attention focused on him.)

After a long pause he gets into how he is sharing his feelings in his new relationship with M. He cries freely off and on during the rest of the hour. He has never done so in therapy before nor has he talked of a loving relationship before. Near the end he says, "I'm growing. It seems hard to believe sometimes."

We both laugh.

- **I make interpretations.**

One of Gendlin's best papers is called "The Experiential Response"(1968). In it he shows how a reflection of feeling response and an interpretation are similar when done experientially.

I am kind of chary in my use of interpretations at least until I have a good rapport with the client. An interpretation is to some extent my telling you something about yourself. This can be tricky. In my experience a lot of people do not like to be interpreted. There is a way to make interpretation least toxic. We will get to that soon.

When I make interpretations, I do not follow one particular school of therapy. I am not a Freudian therapist. Nor a Jungian. Nor a Horneyian. Nor a Gestalt therapist. I do not use just one school's interpretative armamentarium. My interpretations do not come from any one total theory of human growth, development, behavior, and symbolism. My interpretations are directed towards the pre-conceptual richness of the clients' experiencing, now pointing at it from this angle, now from that, now from still another.

Similarly, I do not think in terms of resistance or defenses. If one response of mine doesn't "work," I try another. Or, I try the same one again a little differently or more persistently.

For me, the challenge is always to find the response that reaches my clients *now*, which helps open them to their feelings *now*.

How then do I use interpretations? I give expression to whatever has come to me in response to *this* statement, gesture, or silence of the client. Drawing upon my own reading and therapy experience this may be a Horneyian interpretation, a Sullivanian, or Angyalian, or a T.A. interpretation (*"who* is talking now?"), or a Gestalt interpretation ("be the razor in the dream") or an interpretation from Existential thinking, or in terms of socio-cultural factors.

What do I do after making an interpretation? *This is crucial.* If it is clear that my response has "struck home"—if my client expresses the equivalent of a deep sigh, a "yes," and then something fresh and feel-ingful comes from him—if that happens, we go with what has come.

If not, if my client is silent, or changes the subject, or looks peeved, I want to check in with him. I want to know what my client is experienc-ing and whether and how it relates to my intervention. So as soon as I have a chance, I'll say, "Did *that* comment of mine *say* anything to you?" or "What was that for *you*?" or "What came up in you when I said that?" or "Ok, that was my trip; now where are *you*?"

In this way, even a "wrong" interpretation—poorly timed, off the mark, more true of me than of my client—can be useful. Again, as we saw with self-disclosure and listening, the checking-in is all-important. It keeps me from going on my merry speculative way. I am not invested in the correctness of my interpretation but in finding where my client now is and now wants to go. What will move the process for-ward now—that remains the basic question.

The following example illustrates interpretation and other things that I do. I especially like the example because it also shows how I deal with "chronic therapist wrongness." Orthodox Rogerians sound as if they *always* side with the client. I do so a lot but I don't buy "The client is always right" as an absolute viewpoint.

I have used this example before for another purpose. I come back to it now out of a special fondness for it.

This client was always correcting me. I couldn't listen to her just exactly right. And she demanded exact rightness. The following interaction followed several months of my unstinting efforts to hear her to her satisfaction, efforts that she at times appreciated but which, more often than I am used to, fell short of the mark.

C: You just don't listen well.

T: You're mad at me about that.

C: Yes, mad and disgusted.

T: Mad and disgusted…You know, I'm pretty mad and disgusted with you too. (she looks up) It doesn't feel good to me to be criticized and corrected so much (self-disclosure).

C: I didn't know you felt this way.

T: Well, I do…I've been wondering…Is there anything about you-and-your-father in all this? Something about how he didn't listen to you? (interpretation)

C: (checking this) No…It's more like me-and-my-mother…And it isn't that she didn't listen. (T: Oh) More that she demanded I listen exactly to her!

T: Oh! So I had it wrong…again. (We both laugh.) It's more like you are sometimes doing to me what she did to you. (interpretation)

C: Yes! *That's* it. Hey, you got that one right!

- **Empathetic Imagining**

I want to use this as a separate heading although it is somewhere between guessing, interpreting, listening, intuiting, and self-disclosing.

Sometimes I use my intuition to help a client's experiencing move forward.

I call this kind of response empathetic imagining. I have used this phrase for so long that I do not know whether I made it up or stole it from somewhere.

I feel my way into my clients' worlds to sense where they are at this very minute. I say or express what I imagine to be there.

One place I do this is when a silence is happening. One cannot reflect a silence. One can imagine what it contains.

C: (has been quiet for about four minutes.)

T: I'm looking into your eyes and imagining an infinite sadness there, a pool of grief, and I'm wanting to say—let it out; let me share it with you.

C: (cries) I was remembering my uncle's death.

(C. has told me he is an uptight person. He has been quiet a couple of minutes.)

T: I'm sensing that you're trying to relax

C: Yes.

T: The silence suddenly felt tense to me.

C: Yes. I had been relaxing and then I became aware I was relaxing and tensed up. I'm going to sit quietly and relax some more (silence for five minutes).

C   (sitting quietly, with head dangling down almost guiltily)

T: (after about five minutes) I was just starting to feel like Martha, like I was supposed to reprimand you or something.

C: She never let me have a moment's peace and quiet! I wanted you to break in and I didn't want you to.

T: I was picking up half the message.

C: People tell me I do that.

T: Do what?

C: Invite them to interrupt my solitude.

T: Ah…they tell you that, do they?

C :   Yes. I have to look at how I send out those signals.

Gendlin has written about three categories of in-therapy client behavior which he labels (a) silent and unresponsive; (b) silent but responsive; and (c) verbal but externalized (Gendlin 1967).

As we have seen, I do empathetic imagining especially though not only in response to the first two of these types of behavior. I sit through a silence imagining what this quiet person with me may be feeling and, after what feels to me like a productive silent time, I check out my impression:

T: (The client mumbles something about loneliness. Then he sits silently for a few minutes. I don't want him to be lonely here too. I say softly) I imagine you are feeling quite sad…maybe, cut-off…(no response) maybe, isolated—

C: Yeah. (He starts to cry and goes on to bring up vivid experiences of first loneliness, then sadness, then anger. He becomes quiet again, but it feels like a different kind of quiet. Five minutes or so pass.)

T: I imagine it feels…*good* to share all that with someone—

C: Finally.

T: Finally.

C: Yes, it does. I've held it back a long time. I do feel better now.

I do empathetic imagining in other circumstances too. The person may be talking and suddenly a picture, tune, memory, or physical sensation goes through me. I have learned that when I myself am a particularly empty vessel, particularly clear inside so to speak,(which I am not always) this is my empathetic response to what is in the other person pre-conceptually—just behind, beyond, or below the words being said. I tend to express these imaginings less tentatively. They happen when I'm especially tuned into the client. I would almost say as Mahrer (1978) does, that I am talking from inside the client at these points.[6]

She is talking about an unhappy love affair with an unemployed, alcoholic Sicilian whom she says she wants to leave. I suddenly "see" the Statue of Liberty.

C: (angrily) Why do I care so much for him *still*?

T: "Give me your tired, your poor."

C: (she looks startled and annoyed) What did you say?

T: While you were talking, I saw the Statue of Liberty...the torch...providing shelter for the homeless...

C: (she starts to sob; pause) Is that what I'm doing?

T: Is it?

C: (pause, reflectively, with a slight smile) Strays and waifs...(She nods her head, sighs, and then laughs.)

These experiences of empathetic imagining can be uncanny.

C: (Beginning the session) I don't feel like myself...like I'm together...I feel younger than twenty-seven...I don't feel whole...

T: I don't know what this means, but I just saw the outline of another person's shape as if connected to you on your right-hand side

C: (His mouth falls open; his face takes on an impish, sheepish, young-looking grin.) How did you know I had a twin brother?

T: I didn't!

C: I had a twin brother. We did everything together. When I was fifteen we were suddenly separated...hey, hey, he always walked on my right-hand side. (We both sit there dumbfounded.)

And sometimes—and this is important—I'm wrong:

C: (This is the end of a five-minute, very moving soliloquy. I'm very tuned into him.)...I want to be able to sail on the sea, not be stuck on land. I want to be like Bulkington in Moby Dick and leave the slavish shore. The deeper waters call...

T: (explicating an image that has popped into my consciousness) Is there something about your mother in all this? I say that because I suddenly saw the scene from Interiors...

C: I've seen it.

T: Where the mother drowns and the stepmother saves Jodi's life.

C: It doesn't connect for me. I think it's your stuff.

T: Could be. Just ignore it then…You were saying that deeper waters call.

C: Yeah…I need to take some new steps (continues in same vein)

- **I utilize gestalt role-play methods**

By "gestalt methods" I mean the action experiments developed by Fritz Perls and other gestaltists (Naranjo, n.d.). These are designed to heighten awareness and intensify feeling.

Focusing has been called, jokingly, gestalt for introverts. It emphasizes the inwardness of experiencing. It teaches the client to explore the nuances of his feeling life, to track in loving detail the meandering meanings of inner experiencing. The focuser becomes a virtuoso of felt meanings.

Gestalt is expressive. It is action-oriented. It rolls outward.

The two approaches complement each other. Focusing is a more subtle, assimilative, passive, introverted process. The gestalt experience is more explosive, active, cathartic, extroverted. Zig-zagging back and forth gives the client a full and varied experiencing of himself.

Focusing also stresses the self-directedness of the client more than gestalt does. It makes more person-centered and less abrasive what can be a too directive therapy.

One gestalt technique can be called: "Let me feed you a sentence."

The therapist 'feeds' the client a sentence and invites him to say it himself or change it to how it should have been said or just ignore it if it is entirely wrong.

This is a variation on that method. It is one of my favorite moments in all the therapy I have done.

This is a couples' session. The couple is in their mid-twenties. They have been hemming and hawing about how deep the relationship is and what it means to each of them. It is clear to me that they are right on the edge of a big step.

I say to the man in the couple: "Let's try something."

C: Okay.
T: I am going to feed you two sentences. Say the one that feels most right to Rebecca directly. (Significant pause) "I want to marry you."/"I don't want to marry you."

(Silence)

C: (to me)…Could you leave the room for a little while so we can talk?
T: Sure.

I go to the waiting area and start to read a magazine. After about fifteen minutes he comes and gets me and invites me back into the session.

C: We've decided to get married. It didn't feel right to decide this with you in the room.
T: Fine with me. (The three of us hug).

That was our last couples' session together.

The intra-self dialogue is one of the best—known gestalt methods. Here is how I combined it with focusing and listening in the treatment of the spurned lover we have been following off and on in these chapters:

T: Go see how you are inside right now. (focusing directive)
C: I feel torn apart inside. Part of me says, "Forget him." The other part says, "Go after him."
T: Let those two parts talk to each other. Write a skit. (gestalt directive; I set up two chairs for him to switch between. We have used this method before and I know he takes to it.)
C1   I still want him and I'm going to get him! I'll wait outside his office! (He switches chairs.)

C2   Oh, come off it. Face the facts. He doesn't want you and he's not good for you. You were his slave, remember? Let him go. (switches)

C1   I want to be his slave! Still! Yes! (switches)

C2   Oh, come on. I thought you'd given that crap up. You're still so hung up on winning your father's love? Pshaw! (looks toward me for direction)

T: Now, switch to a third seat, the seat that is yours, Place it wherever between these two feels right and see what's there now. (focusing again)

C: (puts third chair closer to C1 than C2) Longing...Father's face...Father beating me...I still *need* that. (shaking his head ruefully)

T: Be friendly to what still needs that and go see what's the crux of that. (focusing)

C: (teary) That was all I *had* with him...It was our *only* contact...(cries harder)...I know it's crazy but it meant to me— he loves me! (deep sigh)

T: Yeah...so the meaning for you of the beating was—"he loves me" (C: Yeah)...so there's a healthy human longing for love which is coming out in this way...(listening and an Angyalian interpretation, reframing and stressing the healthy trend inside the neurotic symptom)

C: I can see it but I can't feel it. (He is telling me the interpretation makes intellectual but not emotional sense.)

T: You don't feel it the way I said it. (listening)

C: Nah...

T: What's the feeling now?

C: Some sadness and regret! Regret for the wasted years...barking up the wrong tree.

Another example featuring focusing, listening and gestalt:

The outstanding thing for me about this session is that I never learn what specific *content* the person is working on. She works on a feeling.

It changes. She feels better. Neither therapist nor client feels a need to check in with content. (In this and in some other of the examples I will use footnotes to consider alternative responses that could have been used along the way).

The session begins right after a training group exercise in which the background is Nina Simone singing, "I Wish I Knew How It Would Feel to Be Free."

C: I think I want to stay with that music…Everything is so external…

T: You're very focused outwardly and your feelings get lost.[7]

C: Yes, that's right…I don't know if that's good or bad…This is a new place for me.[8]

T: So you feel a little *uncomfortable*…not quite able to decide if it's good or bad.[9]

C: Yeah…I wanted to *feel* the music. I didn't want to be in my head (points to her forehead). It seems like I'm dealing with everything up here right now…

T: You want to be really *feeling* what is going on, and you're somewhat unhappy that you're so much in your head right now. (listening)

C: I'm wondering what I did (voice trails off)…last week it was *all* up here (tapping her forehead again)…I felt so miserable for so many days after…(she seems to be bouncing from thought to thought, leaving each unfinished) retelling gets me in touch…

T: What are you feeling right now? (invitation to focus)[10]

C: Very uncomfortable about the subject…

T: Where in your body do you feel the uncomfortable? (invitation to focus)

C: Right here (puts her fist to her chest).

T: Put your attention right there, and see what that place is saying.

C: "I'm very frustrated." It's saying, "I feel so frustrated!"

T: What do you experience in your body right now? (invitation to focus)

C: A sense of tears coming up (she looks weepy).

T: What does that feel like…just be with that…

C: I feel defeated (she slumps in the chair)…like, it doesn't even pay to think about this problem…I just can't…

T: You're feeling like you just can't deal with it at all…(listening)

C: The frustration is that *it hasn't moved*! (She sweeps away with both her hands)

T: "I'm so *frustrated* with it…" Do that more…(Therapist mirrors client's arm and hand movements) (gestalt)

C: (continues to push away with both her hands) It's old and moldy…I hate it…It's like an old dried up lemon in the back of a refrigerator. (pause)[11]

T: So…like an old, dried up lemon in the back of a refrigerator…old and moldy. (Pause and listening)

C: It sticks in my craw! (Her hands begin to move more vigorously.)

T: Do that again with your hands breathe…Again…more, some verbalization (gestalt)

C: Go away! Get out! Go away! Get out! (Client screams at the thing stuck in her craw. This continues for a few minutes)…I can't believe I did that. It was fantastic!

T: Yeah, *you* were fantastic…

C: …that's what the problem needs—a good screaming at…I'm screaming at my stuckness…

T: What are you feeling right now?[12]

C: (she closes her eyes for a good ten seconds) I'm mourning…the word coming up was "sad"…can I accept that this is the way it is….I'm exhausted.

T: You're mourning the loss of your feelings?[13] (listening)

C: (in response to T's remark) I have lived so long with such rotten feelings…I can't change the situation…I'm *grieving*…

T: You're *grieving*…just let it happen…

C: (sobs for 5 minutes)

T: What are you feeling now?

C: Real good...giggly...I'm in a much better place...I see now that
       I only have to relate to my own expectations and demands, not
       other peoples'...Thanks. [14]

More than one other method can be combined with focusing and listening in the same therapeutic event:

Here are some client's notes on a session from 2/6/85. The example
uses focusing, listening, gestalt and interpretations to help a feeling
move forward and provide profound insights about a piece of troublesome past behavior—a long time spent in bed:

"Started session by saying things had gotten better as I had been
more active, and outside of two days where I had to stay in bed due to
severe cold, was fairly busy. N. suggested that I go inside and see if
anything would come up. (focusing invitation) I did, and was met by
nothing. Finally, it looked as though there was just a small area of sadness, but the rest of the area was all right. Visualized the area as being
cylindrical in shape to the rear of my neck. Felt stuck and complained
of this. N. suggested that I kneel down on the floor and address a large
pillow (where the pillow was to be the sadness that I was trying to
make contact with) (gestalt). I was surprised to see a mass of worms
which were bundled up together and were very active. Rather than
being repulsed by this, I interpreted the mass to mean that it was in
motion and was very entangled and complex. As I tried to relate to the
mass/pillow, the thought that the sadness would always be with me
crossed my mind i.e., that I would always be carrying it around with
me. Its function was to protect me. It was essentially saying, watch out,
be careful. I must be careful. N. was helpful during all of this as he
reflected back to me what I was saying. When the word *convalescing*
came up, tears really began to flow. That certainly was the right word.
It seems that the sadness was using the tears to communicate with me
(my interpretation) to tell me that *convalescing* was indeed the stage
that I was currently in. I concluded that the tears are a way for the sad
part of me, which is there to protect me, to communicate with me, prin-
cipally acknowledgement.

"I tried to interpret my tears in this new light, i.e., a form of communication as opposed to one of self-pity. And that the form, or rather the meaning of the communication, was recognition or acknowledgement that the sadness part was being heard. I also interpreted my long siege in bed as the way that the sad part had chosen to let me heal from a variety of disappointments. All these interpretations—verbalized to N. who simply reflected them back—seemed right on. I could feel them. There was a lot in the session of what N. calls "felt shifts" or "experiential effects." I felt much better and clearer when it was done; my whole long siege in bed felt different now."

In this next example a client is working on his "resistance" to completing a graduate school application. Notice how, through repeated invitations to focus, careful listening, and, towards the end of the transcript, a gestalt dialogue, the whole shape of the problem changes. The gestalt dialogue comes in only after my considerable keeping the client company through focusing and listening. (The next week he finished the application.)

C: I want to talk about my resistance to doing the Columbia application.

T: Some part of you wants to do it, and some part of you is holding out from doing it.

C: Yeah. I'm pretty sure the resistant piece is afraid.

T: The resistance feels like fear.

C: Yeah. I'm afraid I can't say who I am.

T: 'I'm afraid I can't capture myself in words as I am.' Can you touch that fear place inside? (invitation to focus)

C: I don't know much about it.

T: It is *terra incognita*….So, close your eyes, let your attention go to the fear place, just hang out there…Maybe ask, "What is this fear. What's the crux of it?"

C: (after 30 seconds, eyes closed) It feels like an old fear, like I never had confidence in my writing. I didn't know I could write till high school. My inside feeling place still has trouble believing…

T: …early fear.

C: I don't know where it comes from.

T: (taking his cue from C's words) Go inside…make contact again with the fear…Ask it, "Where do you come from?" (invitation to focus)

C: (really perks up!) This is really interesting! I just remembered I was afraid to talk as a child, to say who I was. So it doesn't come from school. I brought it to school. Wow, is that a revelation! I never really knew that.

T: It's a real discovery right now.

C: Yes. The fear is not of writing. The fear is of saying who I am. That feels like a big shift. There is something, though, about writing it down that makes it even scarier.

T: Ah. So there are two steps, not one.

C: Yeah.

T: The first is fear of saying who you are. The second is of writing it down. Could you touch that second fear place? (invitation to focus)

C: (30 seconds) If I write it down, that makes it permanent, and I'll have to live up to it…There is something in there about being right or being wrong.

T: It seems that at the base of the thing about writing is this thing about being right or wrong.

C: Right. Exactly. As if there is a right or wrong…

T: Go inside. Ask, "What is this whole thing about right or wrong?" (invitation to focus)

C: (30 seconds) It's all connected. I just saw it. There is something about not talking in the family and being right or wrong…wait…it's like I have to go through sending the application in and waiting and being judged like by my parents.

T: So, at its crux does the fear…are you saying the fear has to do with your reaction to your parents' being critical of your self-expression?

C: Yeah! That is it right on the nose. Now I've transferred that fear to Columbia.

T: Put your parents right there and talk to them (gestalt instruction)

C: Fuck you! Who do you think you are? You really stifled me. You shouldn't have treated a little kid that way. It was abuse. You made me afraid. You made me keep my beauty and talents inside. You never affirmed me…and now I'm stuck on this sucking application!

T: See what's there now (invitation to focus after gestalt expression)

C: (30 seconds) Some tears for me…how I shut myself up…or down…how I buried my talent in the ground (biblical reference).

T: You shut yourself up—or down—rather than expose yourself to enemy fire.

C: Yeah. But now I have to remember that Columbia is not the enemy.

T: It could be a friend.

C: Yes…And I can do the application!

Kathy McGuire Bowman has been so kind as to publish this example from a demonstration I did in her focusing class[15]. I will quote from her use of it and from my own transcript of the session. It shows mostly focusing and listening and an introduction of a gestalt role-play that the client declines to do, yet I think is important and useful:

"This is a 10-20 minute vignette of focusing therapy (her term) that happened in a classroom demonstration situation. The client is a thirty-year old woman, a graduate student in counseling psychology. The therapist is Neil Friedman…." (McGuire 1991, 240).

C: Um…what I want to talk about…is a feeling that I'm…um…just beginning to recognize…I noticed it yesterday…so I thought, "Great…work on it."

T: So it's kind of like a brand new bud that you noticed blooming just yesterday. (listening)

C: Yeah…but I knew it was coming…it's all around terminating from here [school]…um…with clients…internship…a lot of termination.

T: So, like, you knew it was on the way and you started feeling it just yesterday. (This is just a repetition; it does not add anything at all to what has been said. Probably it slowed things down, which might have helped. At least it did no harm.)

C: Yeah…and it's…there's sadness there…all of this ending…I'm in the graduate program and doing it in one year, it's intense…um…it's kind of like my whole life is here in a lot of ways…it's all going to be over really soon.

T: It's all going to be over really soon (listening)…just let yourself be quiet now and see what's there…(invitation to focus) Let your attention be like a searchlight and go down inside your body…Just breathe into it, just be in a friendly way….

C: (long pause) I can really feel the loss (tearfully) and somehow it has to do with when my mother died.

Kathy comments:
"This is the beginning of a bodily carrying forward. The events around termination at school had touched upon the unresolved grief around mother. The client had not been conscious of this connection at the beginning [of the session], but only conscious of the vague, bodily felt discomfort around the ending…" (p. 242).

We return to the transcript:

T: So the loss of school brings up the loss of mother.

C: (sniffling, tears) Yeah. There's real similarities there. Like she had cancer, and I knew, and I began here right after she died.

T: Um.

C: And I guess it's almost…when you said the words "loss of mother" or "loss of school brings up loss of mother" somehow, I had this whole other sense of how (tearful) nurtured I've felt here.

T: Uh huh.

C: (tearful)

T: The school has been like a mother to you. (interpretation)

C: (more tearful) Yeah…(very tearfully) I'm not ready to lose another one.

T: (softly) Not again. Not another one.

C: (sobbing, sighs) Oh God…now I'm getting more and more connections, like, I realize, I'm graduating in August and I don't recall the exact date, but it's within four days of when she died. I see more and more connection. Losing my mother felt like I also lost my family. I'm the only (more tears) female really left, and she was the link, and kind of without her it's really dissipated…and being here has been a family as well…

T: (Here I shift gears to a Gestalt experiment) Let's try this. (I put three chairs in front of her to represent her mother, the counseling program, and her family.)

C: Oh (very tearfully), that feels like too much to look at all at once. (Cries off and on for several minutes. She does not talk to the chairs, yet I feel the 'experiment' has been a success as it has brought forth still more catharsis. I'm aware we need to stop soon. I wait until her crying subsides on its own.)

C: God…I can't get over it. It feels like the final part of it [the graduation] is going to happen on almost the exact date that I lost her.

T: It almost sounds like somebody planned it.

C: (laughs) Yeah, It kind of feels like it.

T: (aware that time is running out) Could you ask the feeling, "What do you need? What can help things?" Go inside. (invitation to focus)

C: (10 seconds) Well, I got immediately, I need to start therapy again. And to do that now I would have something nurturing, sustaining…that would be…it wouldn't relate to the ending, it would be happening now.

T: Yes, yes.

C: And I really want to do that!

T: Does it feel Ok to stop here? Do you know where to go with this?

C: Yeah, yeah.[16]

A final example: I want to include this one because it adds therapist self-disclosure to the list of kinds of verbal expressions with which focusing invitations and listening responses may be interspersed.

The client is quite recently divorced. I am less recently divorced:

C: I don't know. It is hard getting started.

T: Beginnings are difficult.

C: I meant, in particular, starting over.

T: Oh yes. I remember. 'Here we go again. Pick yourself up, Neil. Off the floor, back out into the world!' (self-disclosure)

C: Yeah. Sort of like that. But for me it is more stumble, get up, stumble; flat on face; get up.

T: (clumsy useless remark) Ram Dass describes his spiritual journey in exactly those terms.

C: But this does not feel very spiritual!

T: I know…for him it may be…but maybe for you it isn't. And maybe my way isn't your way either.

C: I don't have to do it your way?

T: No way! In fact…do it better!
       (We both laugh.)

C: (long pause) I don't know that I can afford that luxury…the luxury you seem to have had of time…

T: Go inside…be gentle with yourself…just ask your inside feeling/knowing place—do I have that kind of time? (invitation to focus)

C: (tears leading into sobs; words between convulsive bodily uprisings) The death thing…too close…no time to waste.

T: (leaves time for him to cry, for me to take this in, for me to be with him compassionately) Maybe you have to do it faster than I did. Check that inside. How does it feel? (invitation to focus)

C: (nodding his head positively) Yeah. Not as an 'ought to,' but as a—'this is the way it is.' There is a given or a belief.

T: Huh?

C: Either it is given or I believe I will die sooner rather than later and I accept that.

T: Acceptance?

C: Yeah. I have to do what I have to do. The time is now.

T: Will you do it? (Notice—a compassionately challenging direct question—another kind of verbal intervention.)

C: (30 seconds) Yes, I will. It helped to hear where you were. It helped to see where I am and have to be, and now I want to be in a different place. By the way, I reserve the right to retrospective reluctance! In other words I may not do it that way at all. But I do intend to move forward.

T: Go for it!

- **Chit-chat**

    We underestimate the role of chit-chat in therapy.

    By chit-chat I refer to what is said before the session formally begins and after it formally ends.

    One fellow told me as he was finishing therapy after much progress that sometimes when I said to him as he went out the door, "hang in there" with a pat on his back, that was the most useful thing he took away from the session.

Another said that our hug at the end of sessions meant a great deal to him; namely, that he could tell me what he considered these awful things about himself, and I was still friendly to him.

The way we are when we greet a client and say good-bye to a client can be as telling as what goes on inside the session itself.

There are a whole slew of interchanges at those times that I would call "ordinary interactions." A. gives me advice on how to get my avocado to grow. I suggest to M. that she read Maya Angelou's autobiography. I make D. a cup of coffee. R. recommends I see *Swept Away*. B. and I discuss the financing of condominiums. L. shows me his sleeping bag. R. and I gossip. B and G and K and I talk about The Red Sox and The Patriots.

In my work, the emphasis on experiencing in therapy exists within the framework of a human relationship in which humor, small talk, simple acts of kindness and shared moments of ordinary interaction also have a place.

Conclusion: I have named and described nine interventions that I make in verbal focusing/listening-oriented therapy: (1) focusing; (2) listening; (3) keeping a client at a feeling place; (4) bringing a client back to a feeling place (5) self-disclosure; (6)interpretations; (7)empathetic imagining; (8) gestalt role-playing;(9) chit-chat before and after the official session.

There is nothing sacred or definitive about these particular interventions. I already see that I have left out pointed questions, which is definitely another part of my repertoire. This has been merely an attempt to show how I combine focusing and listening with several other kinds of verbal interactions. At the time when I was keeping more careful notes and transcriptions of my sessions, I was more into gestalt than I am now. More recent sessions would show more self-disclosure, interpretation, and questions. Exploring this will have to await another publication.

Eight

The Integration of Focusing and Listening and Other Body-Centered Interventions

Now, I want to introduce some therapeutic responses that may be less familiar to you.

In the system of categorization that I use (see below) focusing and listening are body-centered interventions. This may be news to you. After all, many focusing-oriented therapists seldom touch clients' bodies, and mostly Gendlin uses examples for comparison with his own work from client centered and psychoanalytic therapies. Gendlin's Ph.D. is in Philosophy, not Massage.

But, as we shall soon see, focusing and listening are "soft" body-centered interventions. Their aim is to have a bodily felt experiential effect on the client.

One of my favorite Gendlinisms is *"Responses point."*

What does this brilliantly simple sentence mean?

What the therapist says or does points to some part or other of the person.

The therapist's response "why"? points mostly to the intellect. The client's mind is to come up with an answer.

The therapist's response "Tell me more" points to the narrative. The client is to remember what he has been speaking about and continue from where he left off.

The therapist's response, "what does that mean?" can send the client either to mind or to body, depending upon where this particular client looks for 'meaning'.

The therapist's response, "where do you feel that in your body?" points to the body in a focusing way. *It is an invitation to focus.*

Listen to yourself the next time you are with a client. Listen to your responses. To where do they point? How many of your responses point at the client's body and how many of these are in a focusing or listening way? How many point to the head or mind?

Focusing and listening responses point to the body, to the ongoing bodily felt sense in the client. This makes them body-centered interventions.

Much of what follows can be seen as a contribution to and commentary upon Gendlin's Chapter Twelve (Working with The Body: A New and Freeing Energy) and Chapter Sixteen (Emotional Catharsis, Reliving) in Focusing-Oriented Psychotherapy.

Gendlin begins Chapter Twelve by saying that "We have already seen that focusing involves the body. But the body also provides an avenue of therapy" (1996, p.181). He goes on to assert the primacy of the body as he uses the word:

> Please permit me to use the word "body" as the body sensed *from inside* (italics his). Of course, it is the same body that can be observed form outside. And it is more than sensations and observations. Your body feels the complexity of each situation, and enacts much of what you do all day without your needing to think about each move. What you think is of course important, but you can think only a few things at one time. It is your body that totals up the whole situation and comes up with appropriate actions most of the time. Human bodies live immediately and directly in each situation (ibid.).

In another place Gendlin makes clear that other kinds of body-oriented therapists can learn something from focusing just as focusing-oriented therapists can learn from other kinds of body-oriented therapists. I think this is a very good point. It is in that spirit that the following is written.

♦

The body is not just an experiencing process. It is also muscles, arms, legs, feet firmly planted (or not) on the ground. There are other approaches to the body besides Gendlin's. What happens when focusing is combined with interventions that come from these other body-centered approaches?

What do I mean by body-centered interventions?

Robert E. L. Smith, in his 1985 book, *The Body in Psychotherapy* quotes approvingly from Jung: "psyche depends upon body and body depends on psyche."(vii). He goes on to say that "A major trend during the past fifteen years or so has been the bringing of the body into psychotherapy" (Smith 1985, p.iv).

This trend has accelerated since the publication of Smith's book. Bioenergetics, gestalt, yoga, psychomotor, radix, Reichian orgonomy, and, more recently, hakomi, somatic experiencing, EMDR and Asian bodywork—and the combining of these—are now, more than ever, one accepted part of the overall therapeutic landscape. I agree with Smith: "All of these approaches are of value, and not one of them is a complete system having a total perspective on psychopathology, growth, and learning" (1985, vii).

But, when these several approaches are integrated with focusing, then one has what I will call a vibrant and effective body-oriented, focusing-oriented, person-centered experiential therapy.

It is the task of this chapter to describe such a therapy.

Notice that it is the *combining* of methods rather than a monogamous relationship to any one that is characteristic of this approach to therapy. The emphasis in the combining can vary. After introducing the concepts of "hard," "soft," and "expressive" body-centered techniques, Smith writes, "I do a body-oriented Gestalt therapy, integrating aspects of Reichian, neo-Reichian [hard], and other body-focused growth methods in the context of the therapist-patient relationship"

(1985, vii). Whereas I would say I do a focusing-oriented/person-centered, experiential therapy integrating hard, soft, and expressive body techniques along with personal sharings, probing questions, feedback, interpretations, and verbal statements of support and affirmation within the context of a Rogerian-like therapeutic relationship.

◆

There is no universally agreed-upon system of categorization of body-oriented therapeutic methods. I like the classification introduced in Smith's book. He talks of "soft," "hard" and "expressive" body-centered techniques. I want to take them up in turn, define and describe several examples of each, and show some ways to combine them with focusing and listening.

First, though, a digression into the history of touch in psychotherapy.

I will keep this brief. Some points have to be made because touch is such a controversial topic in the therapeutic world (Smith, Clance, and Imes 1998). These authors say that:

> Shrouded for many in a cloak of fear, rumor and misinformation, touch is perhaps the most controversial subject in psychotherapy today…therapists express fear of being misunderstood if they touch clients and then being vulnerable to ethical or even legal charges" (ibid., xi).

I would assent that there are oodles of fear in therapists (perhaps especially those in private practice) from a number of angles, all of which come down to the possibility of being sued or otherwise abused by clients who are overbearingly unhappy with their therapy. In our litigious society, this fear is far from baseless. There is danger though in being ruled by it. Judicious use of touch is called for.

◆

Of "soft" techniques, Smith writes that they "tend to be gentle and allowing rather than forcing…[they] tend to be subtle. The things which happen, such as increased body awareness, psychological regression, increased experience of emotion, and expression of emotion, do not happen as quickly or as dramatically [as with the other two categories]…the soft methods are safe…." (p. 115).

Hakomi probes, work with posture and light touching, and work with the breath are examples of "soft" technique. {See Table 1.} Tables are based on material in Smith (1985).

Table 1—Soft Technique

Characteristics:	gentle and allowing
	subtle
	safe
	may or may not include physical touch
Results	increased body awareness
	psychological regression
	increased experience of emotion
	expression of emotion
	contact, empathy, nourishment
	access and deepening of inner experience
Examples:	Posture
	Touch
	Breathing
	Listening
	Focusing
	hakomi probes
	guided inner experience

I want to illustrate the combining of focusing with (1) touch and (2) hakomi probes.

- **Focusing and Touch[1]**

Focusing-oriented therapy that includes touch grows naturally out of Gendlin's focusing/listening therapy. It was Gendlin's discovery that certain words, phrases, and images have an "experiential effect." When they are said by the client—or said back to the client by the therapist—they carry experiencing forward. The "talk therapist" tries to say such words. He directs his verbal articulations at the felt sense of the client. When his words "hit the mark," so to speak, verbal therapy moves forward.

It is only a small step to "hands on" body therapy. The link: Focusing involves the body. The felt sense is in the body. It is real. It is bodily felt. What distinguishes verbal focusing therapy from "just talking" (or "just imagery") is that it is bodily.

Since focusing is bodily, it makes sense that the focusing therapist could make use also of other body-centered interventions.

For example, the "body-oriented focusing therapist" uses touch to:

- Anchor the felt sense
- Amplify the felt sense
- Help the felt sense to move

Anchoring the felt sense: The client has identified a felt sense in her chest. "It's here," she says, pointing to her chest. With her permission, the therapist places her hand gently on the place the client has pointed to. This helps anchor the felt sense. It helps the client stay focused. The therapist's hand says, "Keep your attention right here."

Clients who are focusing do have difficulty in keeping their attention on the felt sense. This is a real problem. They lose it. They wander. They get distracted. They talk about the weather. The therapist, by putting a hand on the felt sense, can help keep the client "on beam"—tuned into the felt sense.

However, it is crucial that the therapist's touch be non-erotic and removed if it seems to be interfering rather than helping with the client's process.

Amplifying the felt sense: The therapist's touch also helps by increasing the "volume" of the felt sense. Rub your hands together. Feel the energy.

When the therapist touches the place where the felt sense is, she sends energy directly to it. This can amplify the felt sense, especially if the touch is not experienced as intrusive.

For example, during focusing a client said he had a pressure in his stomach. The therapist asked if he could put his hand on the client's stomach. (Notice this "asking" way of introducing touch.) The client said yes. The therapist placed his hand on the client's stomach, waited, and then asked, "What are you experiencing?" The client responded, "The pressure feels sharper, clearer. I can sense it better."

Helping the felt sense move: The therapist can use her touch to help the felt sense move. When a felt shift comes at the end of a round of verbal focusing therapy, some way that the body has been carrying its troubles actually changes. It seems miraculous, at first, that words, distal as they are, can do this. Not surprisingly, touch, properly applied, can do it, too.

For example, the client's felt sense was something pushing down on his chest. The word for it was "burdened." The therapist repeated the word, "burdened" The client said, "Yes! Exactly. On my chest, burdened." The therapist used his touch to "imitate" the felt sense. He pushed down—hard—on the client's chest. The client reported he felt some "give" inside. Then, as the therapist continued to push, he gave the client the instruction, "Let your body do what it wants to do." The client pushed back against the therapist—that is, against the external imitation of the felt sense. The therapist pushed back. The client got angry. The therapist and client were soon wrestling. The client threw the therapist (i.e. the burden) off. "That feels better," the client reported. A big shift had occurred. The client felt lighter, energized, exhilarated, clear. With the burden off he now "saw" that he needed to mobilize his anger under his depressed/burdened place. The insight had come after the shift, just as focusing theory would predict.

In sum, I am suggesting an addition to focusing/listening therapy in the direction of touch. The body-oriented therapist does everything that the verbal therapist does. He also uses his or her touch to help anchor, amplify, and move the felt sense.

- **Hakomi Probes and Focusing**

A second "soft" technique is the Hakomi probe.

Hakomi purports to be a complete system of body-centered psychotherapy. (See Kurtz 1994) It was begun by Ron Kurtz who was influenced by Al Pesso, Moshe Feldenkrais, and Eastern principles of non-violence and mindfulness.

Turning away from the hard and forcing nature of his training in bioenergetics, Kurtz and his original trainees developed a body-centered therapy that combines a background of Eastern teachings with a Rogerian respect for the person and powerful body-oriented interventions.

A Hakomi probe is the kind of statement an ideal parent would make. For example, "You are perfectly welcome here"…"Your needs are Ok…" "You are fine just the way you are'…" Everything is going to be all right."

The Hakomi therapist delivers the probe in a ritualized way. He gets the person into mindfulness, eyes closed, attention inside his own present experiencing. (This is very akin to focusing.) Then, he puts his hand on the client's chest, says his first name, and very slowly delivers the probe: "Al, you are perfectly welcome here…". He may repeat it—with the person's name—three times. Then he asks for the person to report his experience.

Here is how I combine focusing with a Hakomi probe:

He has been talking about his distrust of people in general. The talking has started "off the top of his head" but has moved closer to feeling:

T: What are you feeling right now? Go inside. *(invitation to focus)* Let your attention come down into your body. See if there is a word, phrase, image, sound, or gesture for what's there.

C: It's funny. I'm feeling like I trust you!

T: Ha! A surprise. You trust me.

C: Yeah, but don't get cocky…I don't trust M, Z, or B! They aren't going to pull anything over on me.

T: Let's try something. (Client nods Ok) Close your eyes. Breathe. Put your attention right here under the palm of my hand—is it Ok if I put my hand here? (Client nods yes) Now, pay attention to what you experience when I say these words: 'Charlie, all people are your friends…Charlie, all people are your friends…Charlie, all people are your friends…'

Now, what happened?

C: (He had begun to cry on my second repetition of the probe.) I felt my *longing* to believe that. I know you've said things like that before. But I never really felt—I want to believe it! So just now I felt the wanting, the yearning…and also that I can't (sob)…I just can't.

T: Focus again. Be friendly to yourself. Ask yourself, "Why not? Why can't I believe it? Don't ask it judgmentally…but with real caring for yourself."

C: (deep sobbing) Because they [his parents] beat me too much, and they were the first ones. The first models weren't my friends. I can't get beyond that—yet.

T: You can't get beyond that—yet. (listening)

C: Yes, but I did feel—there is some hope. It could shift.

Here is another example. I cannot overstate how valuable the combination of focusing and Hakomi probes is:

She has been talking about how she lives for others; how she doesn't take care of herself; how she is all worn out. The talk has been getting more and more feelingful:

T: Let's try something.

C: Ok.

T: First, just go inside and see how you are right now (*invitation to focus*)

C: (closes her eyes, takes 30 seconds, tunes in to herself) I'm pretty Ok, sort of full of feeling, but calm, serene, even though I'm really feeling what I've been saying.

T: Ok. Now keep your attention inside. If it's Ok, I'm going to put my hand here on your chest (Client nods Ok). Put your attention right under the palm of my hand and now just listen inside and report to me what happens when I say…'Chris, your needs are Ok'…Chris, your needs are Ok…Chris, your needs are Ok….

What happened?

C: That was fantastic
T: Yeah…but what happened?
C: I saw the house I grew up in. I saw my parents in separate rooms…away from each other. I saw my four brothers all involved in doing things…and I saw—no one had any time for me! I even went from room to room trying to make contact (she cries here), but no one stopped what they were doing; no one paid any attention—
T: To your needs.
C: Right! And they still don't. I go home and it is the same story. Damn! To this day I'm invisible.
T: You live your life as if everyone were your family. (interpretation)
C: What do you mean?
T: As if your needs are unimportant to us all…
C: And, therefore, to myself! Damn. I'm going to change that.
T: You really have to, you know, or you are going to wear yourself out and ruin your health. (feedback, said lovingly)
C: (cries) I don't want to admit it—but you're right.

Notice that Hakomi and focusing are quite similar. There is only a slight change in the energetic vibration of the session as one moves from focusing to a Hakomi probe. They combine easily together and carry the session forward on a similar wavelength.[2]

As focusing and listening are themselves examples of "soft" technique, its combination with other "soft" techniques does not much change the overall feel of the session.

Our next examples of "hard" techniques will be quite different.

◆

By "hard techniques" Smith refers to methods of body intervention which are neither subtle nor gentle. They may be, in fact, uncomfortable and painful. They "tend to be dramatic in their releasing of blocked emotion and memories." They are of "high potency and therefore require considerable judgment and caution…if they are to be used in growthful rather than traumatic ways" (1985 chap. 9). They can contribute mightily to unblocking and disinhibiting. They are dramatic and their incorrect use can be traumatic.

This latter needs reinforcing. These are not methods to mess around with. (Don't try them out at home!) They can do real harm. I would be very chary in their usage although I do believe that they sometimes give results that may be much more difficult to achieve without them.

Smith discusses hard techniques from Reichian, bioenergetic, and psychomotor therapy (see Table 2).

Table 2—Hard Technique

Characteristics:	neither subtle nor gentle
	can be uncomfortable/painful
	can be dramatic
	high potency/high risk
	force/pressure
	use with care
Results:	dramatic breakthroughs
	release of blocked emotions/memories
	disinhibition
	resumption of flow
Examples:	deep pressure on various muscles (Reich)
	"limits structure" (Pesso)
	mimicking "hard" feelings inside body (Focusing)

The flavor of Reichian hard technique—what it is like, what the client thinks of it, what it accomplishes—is most charmingly captured in this long excerpt from Orson Bean's *Me And The Orgone*. Bean describes his first session with Reichian therapist, Dr. Baker, who has just finished some opening chit-chat with him. I quote this at length as it beautifully captures the flavor of a kind of work that is not all that well known even inside the body therapy community:

> Dr. Baker sat down behind his desk and indicated the chair in front of it for me...."Well," he said, "take off your clothes and let's have a look at you." My eyes went glassy as I stood up and started to undress—"You can leave on your shorts and socks," said Baker, to my relief. I laid my clothes on the chair against the wall in a neat pile, hoping to get a gold star. "Lie down on the bed," said the doctor. "Yes, sure," said Willie the Robot, and did so. "Just breathe naturally," he said pulling a chair over to the bed and sitting down next to me. I fixed my eyes on a spot of water damage near the upper left-hand corner of Dr. Baker's window and breathed naturally. I thought: "What if I get an erection, or shit on his bed or vomit." The doctor was *feeling the muscles* (italics mine) around my jaw and neck. He found a tight cord in my neck, pressed it hard and kept on pressing it. It hurt like hell but Little Lord Jesus no crying he makes. "Did that hurt?" asked Dr. Baker.
>
> "Well, a little," I said, not wanting to be any trouble
>
> "Only a little?" he said.
>
> "Well, it hurt a lot," I said. "It hurt like hell."
>
> "Why didn't you cry?"
>
> "I'm a grown-up."
>
> He began *pinching the muscles* in the soft part of my shoulders. I wanted to smash him in his sadistic face, put on my clothes and get the hell out of there. Instead I said "Ow." Then I said "That hurts.
>
> "It doesn't sound as if it hurts," he said.

"Well, it does," I said, and managed an "Oooo, Oooo."

"Now breathe in and out deeply," he said and he placed the palm of one hand on my chest and pushed down hard on it with the other. The pain was substantial. "What if the bed breaks?" I thought. "What if my spine snaps or I suffocate?

I breathed in and out for a while and then Baker found my ribs and began probing and pressing.

I thought of Franchot Tone in the torture scene from *Lives of a Bengal Lancer*. I managed to let out a few pitiful cries which I hoped would break Baker's heart. He began to jab at my stomach, prodding here and there to find a tight little knotted muscle. I no longer worried about getting an erection, possibly ever, but the possibility of shitting on his bed loomed even larger. He moved downward, mercifully passing my jockey shorts. I don't know what I had expected him to do, measure my cock or something, and began to pinch and prod the muscles of my inner thighs. At that point I realized that the shoulders and the ribs and the stomach hadn't hurt at all. The pain was amazing, especially since it was an area I hadn't thought would ever hurt. Notwithstanding, my feeble vocal expressions were nothing that would have shamed Freddie Bartholomew.

"Turn over," said Baker. I did and he started at my neck and worked downwards with an *unerring instinct for every tight, sore muscle*. He pressed and kneaded and jabbed and if I were Franchot Tone I would have sold out the entire Thirty-first Lancers. "Turn back over again," said Dr. Baker and I did. "All right," he said, "I want you to breathe in and out as deeply as you can and at the same time roll your eyes around without moving your head. Try to look at all four walls, one at a time, and move your eyeballs as far from side to side as possible." I began to roll my eyes, feeling rather foolish but grateful that he was no longer tormenting my body. On and on my eyes rolled. "Keep breathing," said Baker. I began to feel a *strange pleasurable feeling in my eyes* like the sweet fuzziness that happens when you smoke a good stick of pot. The fuzziness began to spread through my face and head and then down into my body. "All right," said Baker. "Now I want you to continue breathing and do a *bicycle kick* on the bed with your legs." I began to raise my legs and bring them down rhythmically, striking the bed with my calves. My thighs began to ache and I wondered when he would say that I had done it long enough, but he didn't. On and on I went, until my legs were ready to drop off. Then, gradually, it didn't hurt anymore and that same sweet fuzzy sensation of pleasure began to spread through my whole body, only much stronger. I now felt as if a rhythm had taken over my kicking which had nothing to do with any effort on my part. *I felt transported and in the grip of something larger than me. I was breathing more deeply than I ever had before and I felt the sensation of each breath all the way down past my lungs and into my pelvis.* Gradually, I felt myself lifted right out of Baker's milk chocolate room and up into the spheres. I was breathing to an astral rhythm. Finally, I knew it was time to stop. I lay there for how many minutes I don't know and I heard his voice say, "How do you feel?"

"Wonderful," I said. "Is this always what happens?"

"More or less," he said. "I can see you on Tuesdays at two. Ideally I'd like to see you twice a week but I don't have the time and once a week is more than sufficient."

I stood up shakily and began to pull on my clothes. "I'm a bit dizzy," I said.

"You'll be all right," he said. "Just take it easy. Actually you're in pretty good shape. It shouldn't take too long."

We agreed on a price per hour, I finished dressing, shook his hand and walked out into the waiting room. A bald-headed man sat there reading *Life* magazine. He didn't look up. I wondered how long he had been there and if he had heard my noises in the other room. I walked out the door and down the hall. It seemed as if my feet barely touched the carpeted halls.

I came out into the air and crossed the street into the park. I looked up into the sky over the East River. It was a *deeper blue* than any I had seen in my life, and there seemed to be little flickering pinpoints of light in it. I looked at the trees. They were a *richer green* than I had ever seen. It seemed as though *all my senses were heightened.* I was perceiving everything with *greater clarity.* I walked home feeling *exhilarated* and *bursting with energy.* That night I went to work at the theater and got through the show somehow. I didn't know if I was good or bad. I got home sometime after midnight and I knew there was no remote possibility of going to sleep. Far from settling down, the energy coursing through my body had increased as the night went on, moving rhythmically up and down from head to toe. There was no doubt in my mind that it was *orgone energy* or whatever the hell name anyone wished to give it. It was like nothing I had ever felt before and I knew that I had tapped into the strongest force in the world. I sat by my window on the river, watching the debris float by. I thought about life and people and kids and sex and my ex-wife and psychoanalysis and how in the name of God human beings had gotten themselves into the shape they were in and finally, about five-thirty in the morning, I fell asleep (Bean, 31-36).

Let me say right away that I don't have clients take off their clothes and that the eye-rolling segment and bicycle kick segment are soft and expressive techniques rather than hard techniques. But most of the session is a good example of Reichian hard techniques described quite beautifully. Notice both Bean's comments on what the client is saying to himself *during* the work (an equivalent of—what is this shit!), and how he feels after (an altered state of ecstatic consciousness). Both the client's inner comments on his experience of hard technique *and* the remarkable after-effects of hard technique need to be given careful, respectful, and due consideration. There can be no doubt that something very powerful has happened here[3]

One might think that the combination of focusing and hard technique is unlikely. After all, Dr. Baker does not sound like a focusing therapist! He sounds like just the opposite, just the kind of therapy and therapist focusing is the antidote for!

Yet, empirically, it turns out that focusing and hard technique *can* be combined. This is surprising. Even with its philosophical opposite—violent, therapist-directed, pushing—there can be combining. This is an important point.

If focusing work is the ground, the foundation upon which therapy sits, then moments of hard technique combined with focusing are quite possible: The combination is *very* powerful. Consider these examples:

C: When I close my eyes and go inside I feel like throwing up. There is an image of a hand over my mouth, keeping me from speaking.

T: May I do that?

C: (surprised) What?

T: (matter-of-factly) Put my hand over your mouth. I'll try to do it like it is in the image. (Notice that I ask permission to initiate hard technique.) Let me know when I get it right, if you want to do it. Then, breathe…and let your body do whatever it wants to do. Ok?

C: (a bit warily) Ok.

T: (puts hand over client's mouth; adjusts force until C nods head "yes" as in "yes, that's it.")

C: (muffled)

T: Let your body do whatever it wants to do.

(At first C collapses. I keep my hand over her mouth. For about a minute she is rolled up in a fetal-like ball. I am leaning over her with my hand over her mouth. She signals to stop. I take my hand away.)

C: It's moved. It's in my throat now, squeezing at me.

T: May I?

C: (gives me an "oh my God, this too?" look) Sure.

I put my hand over her neck and squeeze—not as hard as I can, but hard enough. Suddenly, she starts to stir and to fight. She grabs at my hand to pull it away from her neck, and I don't let her.

T: No you don't. Keep it in. I won't let you out. (By now we are in a violent tussle rolling around the room—this is in my private office, and it is rather large. We keep wrestling for a few minutes until she finally uses both her hands and all her force and pulls at my bracelet…and gets me to let go. We lay a few feet apart from each other. She is crying and laughing wildly. I am laughing.)

In exchange for a reduction in fee, this client wrote me two or three pages of her reflections on each session. Hence, we have her own words about this interaction.

"6/16/88—The neck thing was interesting. Actually, I knew the block has been there for a very long time…on and off since I was about sixteen. Maybe even way before that.

"Interesting that when Neil held his hand hard over my mouth…I felt it familiar and bearable (on one level). If that is what you [her partner] want to do to me, why resist? And then as I tried to take his hand away…I really didn't! I thought about pushing it away, and it felt premature, like, I'm not ready. It is as if I don't want to come out mean and harsh and bad! Some part of me at sixteen pulled back…the sexuality part…and became held in and has been there all this time…

"And then when Neil started to press hard against my neck…it was different from my mouth. Ah ha! You want to squeeze the life out of me! That I will not take!

"That is when I pushed his hand away. Hard.

"So I'm willing to be shut up in a relationship, but not to give up my life. Interesting…I felt Ok during the session. I'm ready to move, to get unstuck."

Here is another example of focusing and hard technique. Remember: much of the background of our sessions are focusing, listening, and other verbal methods. What I am highlighting, however, are some of the breakthrough sessions which sometimes combine focusing with other, quite different kinds of body-centered techniques.

This is another session that this client wrote up for me:

"2/21/89—When I went in I didn't know what I wanted to work on. Neil gave me focusing instructions. I wasn't anxious—which I've been feeling lately—but I could feel something pushing out—and being held from within at the same time.

"Feel that," said Neil. Definite bondage. And since it was being held from within, I knew I had everything to do with it. I felt it particularly in my legs! That was new. It had something to do with who I am and who I am not. A lot of weight on my legs…

"Neil sat on my legs. Hard. It felt normal. So I pushed him off (I'm glad I'm as big as he is!) not really knowing why I did. Then I was suddenly sobbing and crying. Out of nowhere. This went on for maybe five minutes.

"After the tears, the insights: Like this is my facade, but I won't tolerate you really believing this is who I am. I mean the wanting to be liked. It isn't who I really am. Where does this whole thing about being liked really come from, and why is it so important to me? It is like a dead weight holding me down [on my legs] so I cannot move. I mean, it is an overwhelming factor in my relationship with the world.

"Near the very end of the session…my legs felt very different [felt shift]…I don't mean just from getting his weight off them…I mean from the inside. I started to get the feeling…maybe I am getting ready to move."

Another example of focusing and hard technique: This one comes from an Opening The heart workshop. It is a seven-minute segment of work with a participant in the workshop. (This one has elements of hard and expressive technique, which we will take up next).

T: Go inside and see what is there.
C: (after 30 seconds) I don't know if I can tell you.
T: You don't know if you can tell me. (Listening)
C: The image is so horrible…and I have it so often.
T: There is a horrible image there, one you have quite frequently. (Listening)
C: Yeah…Ok…I see myself holding a knife and stabbing myself in the stomach with it. The feeling with the image is—disgust. But it is what I want to do.
T: Would you be willing to try something?
C: (looks at me warily) Maybe.
T: Make a fist like you are holding a knife in your hand. (C does this) Then, let me grab you by the wrist. (She agrees) Now, you try to stab yourself, and I'll hold you back. I'll make sure you don't do it. (In Hakomi terms, this is an example of "taking over")
C: Are you sure you can keep me from doing it?
T: I'm sure…but we can try it for a minute so you'll see
C: Let's try it.

We try it out. She struggles to "stab" herself. I am able to keep her from doing so. We stop.

C: Ok, you can do it. I'm game.

I ask her to wait a minute while I go down to the kitchen. I get a relatively blunt-edged butter knife and come back upstairs to her and give it to her.

T: See how you are inside right now
C: Excited!
T: Ok, whenever you are ready.

She tries to stab herself and I stop her. I also verbalize what I imagine are the voices she hears when she has this image: "I want to be dead. Life isn't worth it. I want out." I scream these words, and she throws herself more and more into the self-destructive effort. She pulls me all around the room...but she never "stabs" herself. Her face looks fiercely angry, and I hold her wrist very hard. After seven minutes the bell rings, and we fall to the ground—three-quarters of the way across the room—in a heap.

The rest of the morning she was very alive and present. She thanked me twice for the experience. I had never seen her so relaxed as I did later that day.

One more example. This, too, is from the Heart workshop. It is similar to the example I used in the focusing and touch section.

T: What is happening inside you? (*invitation to focus*)
C: There is all this tension...I'm carrying it on my neck and shoulders
T: Can I be the tension?
C: What do you mean?
T: Get on your knees. (C does this) I'll get on your neck and shoulders with my hands leaning on you like the tension does.
C: Oh, I see, Ok, why not?

I lean all my weight on the palms of my two hands digging into his neck and shoulders. At the same time I tell him to breathe and to let his body do whatever it wants. He is a little smaller than me, and I am feeling very powerful and energetic this morning. He starts to struggle and fight to get out from under the pressure (me)…and I won't let him.

C: Wait a minute.

He takes off his glasses. Now, he really goes at it. I'm yelling, "You can't get out from under me," and he's yelling, "I'll get you off me you son-of-a-bitch." We wrestle and roll around the floor…and just as he throws me off…I climb right back on—just as I imagine his pressure does. We are back at it again, maybe for five minutes altogether, and in the end we are laughing uncontrollably after he does, for good, throw me off.

C: My shoulders sure feel better!
T: How about *you*? How are you? How are you inside? *(invitation to focus)*
C: I feel exhilarated! I haven't had so much fun in years. And I feel relaxed—boy, do I put a lot of pressure on myself. But it is not there now. I really see how I do it to myself, and how I have to stop doing it to myself.
T: Will you?
C: Time will tell.
T: Yes. It always does.

We hug.

I want to repeat. *I do not use hard techniques often. Focusing and listening are the staples of my therapy. But the care-full use of hard technique can really propel things forward. I emphasize 'care-full'. I am quite good at these methods and thus have confidence in my usage of them.*

♦

Smith says that "the essence of the expressive techniques is taking action, concrete musculoskeletal movement." He adds, "the action to be growthful, however, must carry symbolic meaning" (Smith 1985, 135).

The expressive techniques, then, involve the client's taking symbolic action beyond the point of usual self-interruption. "The expressive work involves movement of energy into the musculoskeletal system...support is given to the patient's acting on what he or she is organismically experiencing as growthful or natural, rather than self-interrupting and continuing the old pattern of avoidance. The patient is invited and encouraged to act in spite of the voice of the toxic introject, to act in the face of catastrophic expectation" (Smith, ibid.).

Much psychotherapeutic expressive work is verbal, and Smith singles out the gestalt therapy literature for this (I would agree and add the psychodramatic.) Smith makes the case forcefully for the need for body-oriented expressive work to really finish the unfinished business:

> When there is self-interruption, there is some body part that has not been put to full use. There are an arm and fist that have not hit, a jaw that has not bitten, tear glands which have not secreted, a throat which has not screamed, a belly which has not chuckled, a pelvis which has not thrust...expressive work involves the reowning of the 'missing' body part (Smith, p. 136).

Focusing and expressive work were made for each other. One is the inner act; the other is the outer act. They make a good gestalt.

Gendlin explicitly acknowledges the need to combine focusing with expressive techniques:

> Many events, especially in childhood, generate strong emotions and at the same time block their expression. If a child can cry, shake, and scream, it is sooner done with a painful event. But along with bad events children are usually also prohibited from expressing anything [that the parent or care-giver does not want to hear]. One meaning of 'completing' an incomplete experience is to let these long-missing expressive sequences happen (Gendlin 1991, 265).

Another kind of completion concerns the interaction: what one could not tell the original people, how one could not fight back. Incomplete interactions need to be completed…in therapy there needs to be room and welcome to cry the uncried tears, to sob, shake, or move to express old pain and fury in more than words (ibid.).

Therapy must involve more than focusing on inner data in reflective inner space. There also needs to be a movement outward, into interaction….Moving out, rolling out [his term for expressive action] is an essential dimension of therapeutic change that is not provided by inward process dealing only with inner data (Gendlin, ibid., 267).

I do not feel that Gendlin goes far enough in providing for this expressive rolling out. He says:

Cathartic therapists are right to tell other therapists not to stop expressive discharge, however, intense it may be…I welcome discharge when it has already come. The next question is whether it should be deliberately engendered…On that question agreement is not so easy, and I am not sure of the way I have chosen…*I believe that catharsis should be an open, known, and included possibility. Beyond that I don't believe I should engender it. (italics mine)* (Gendlin 1991, 265-266).

My own experience both in private practice and group workshops is that clients often need a lot of encouragement and cheerleading in order to get into cathartic, expressive, or intense feeling work. The work is unusual. It breaks certain taboos. It can be scary. It can seem strange. Weird. It requires trust. It breaks culturally internalized lessons ("Don't ever raise your voice at me"; "big boys don't cry"; "big girls don't hit.") In my experience, if the therapist really wants expressive work to happen, he has to lend it his energy wholeheartedly, have props available, and also find a way that helps each particular client feel safe in it. Simply mentioning that it exists as an option is not, in my experience, enough. The dice are too loaded against *intense expressive emotional release*. The therapist needs to "point" the client towards it.

Here are several examples in which focusing and expressive work are combined. I want to say that some of the following (and preceding) work in this chapter may strike some of you as either miracle cures or snake oil fakes. They are more likely closer to the former than the latter.

He is from the Middle East and grew up with a tyrannical father who physically and emotionally abused himself and his eight siblings. Whenever any one of them had done something the father deemed wrong—which included a shifting list of many items—all eight would be paddled on their behinds as punishment.

My client is a fifty year-old quite accomplished professional who feels that he is still held back by the results of this tyrannical treatment by his father.

I invite him onto the futon I have in my office. We have never used it before. I have him take off his shoes and sit on a backjack, and I show him a bataka and explain its use.

I have him close his eyes. I lead him in a visualization where he will see a blank movie screen and then the words "Scenes from Me and My Father's Relationship" appear on the screen. I invite him to slowly savor each scene that comes up. Slowly, I lead him into stepping into the movie and really beginning to let form in his body the feelings that he is having as he watches the movie.

I should say that I am particularly warmed up to this kind of work with him today and that he is a very highly motivated and in the best sense of the word compliant client. He will try new things out.

I tell him that when he opens his eyes I will be sitting across form him and facing him. He is to put on my face the face of his father. That is, when I ask him, "Tell me how you feel about me", he is to respond to me as if I were his father and were inviting him to talk in this way honestly.

He opens his eyes and says, "I feel angry at you." I let him say some examples of what he is angry about. Then, I introduce the bataka and demonstrate how to get a good stretch (bioenergetics) as he brings the bataka held with both hands back over his head and then whacks it onto a large pillow I have put between us and invited him to see his father's face on.

I should say that I also explain that this is "symbolic expressive work" and does not mean he is to do this outside of the therapy office to anyone!

He starts. He is really into it. He whacks away. I cheerlead. "Go for it! Really give it to him! Remember the beatings! Use sound! Say words! Say the worst words!"

I am entirely on his side and he can feel that.

After awhile he stops and reports a tingling at the base of his spine which then comes right up his backbone and like a shroud out and over his face. He is amazed at what has just happened.

I invite him to focus. This is important. This is where the focusing comes in. What does he feel in his body now? "Lighter". His face lights up with his beautiful but seldom present smile. He breaks out laughing. It is a laughter of liberation and glee. I have never seen him this way before. I ask him to check inside and see if he wants to do it again. He does. More of the same until he is tired and stops and smiles and laughs and talks more about him and his father.

He is going home. It is Seven P.M. I suggest that he carefully monitor his inner life for the next few days. I expect that there will be more changes. I tell him that the energy that he has released is sometimes called Kundalini energy. I would call if life-forward energy and I tell him that it is quite trustworthy and not dangerous.

When we hug it is the hug of two comrades in the trenches celebrating a victory.

I cannot wait to see him the next week!

This next example is one of my all-time favorites. Both for aesthetic reasons and in terms of its overall effect it seems to me picture-perfect.

The context was a Heart workshop in which there are what we call "healing circles". Laury Rappaport was doing the overall timing of all the healing circles. I was leading one.

I had worked some earlier with this woman. She had made reference to a terrible trauma when she was eleven years old. Her mother had set fire to her favorite doll's clothes. She mentioned especially a Barbie's blue dress.

When she lay down on the mat for her healing circle she mumbled that she wanted to work on "the Barbie dress thing." I asked her to close her eyes and tell me what she felt (*invitation to focus*). She said, "apprehensive, scared, terrified."

I asked her to keep her eyes closed and, speaking in the present (gestalt) tell me the story of the doll dress.

She began: "I'm eleven years old. I'm sitting on the porch playing with my Barbies. My mother has just come home from the crazy hospital. She is upset about something. She sees my Barbies. My favorite has on a blue dress."

At this point, as she is talking, I signal to Laury, "bring over the old blue bataka that is falling apart and a box of matches." Laury doesn't know exactly what is going on, but she catches my drift and brings over the props.

Back to the story:

"Mother is mad at me for some reason. She tells me she is going to get rid of my doll clothes." (The story is told with increasing agitation.) "I cry and beg her not to, but she grabs my Barbie and takes off the blue dress. Then, she takes a match...."

At this point I have Laury stand above her with a lighted match about to touch the old blue bataka.

"And she sets fire to the blue dress."

At this point I instruct the woman to open her eyes and look straight up. At this moment Laury sets the bataka on fire.

The woman makes a piercing shriek that is heard throughout the workshop room above the din of everyone else. She loses it. She is moaning and groaning and moving all around, and I get down real close to her to keep her company. This goes on for five minutes. The group surrounds her lovingly but also gives her room as she screams, yells, punches, and kicks. Finally, as she seems to settle down I invite her to talk directly to her mother (Laury), who has been standing there the whole time.

"How could you have done that? Why were you so sick?

"I hadn't done anything bad (tears). That was my favorite dress. That Barbie was my real friend (sobs). You burned her favorite dress. What kind of a mad woman were you?"

She continues to cry for another five minutes, those old, ancient, forbidden tears; and then, by the time the bell rings, she is quiet, taking in the love from the women around her through a laying on of hands. Her face is transformed. She is glowing. I feel a very full contentment.

In a letter after the workshop she thanked us profusely and told us of the real life changes she made in the following week. They were many and included—buying herself a Barbie with a blue dress!

The next example also comes from a healing circle at a Heart workshop. (I think it ought to be said that the Opening The Heart workshop was an absolutely ideal place to practice this kind of work. Although as of 1997 Spring Hill no longer exists there are still Heart workshops at Omega and Kripalu centers.)

It was a men's workshop, and I had in my circle five men who had known each other for some time. Two were twins. They asked if they could take a turn together.

I said yes. They told me they wanted to re-enact their birth. (They were both quite "warmed-up" and had previously done considerable work individually and together in psychotherapy.)

I had them lay on a mattress and had a second mattress placed over them. The group held the second mattress in place—not forcefully—just enough for it to be womb-like.

They both must have been inside there about five minutes. There was no big noise—just little whimpering sounds. One (the older by five minutes) started to come out through an opening we gradually gave him at one end of the mattress. He cried, like a baby, and the group held him.

Then, there were moans and movements and crying from inside. The other twin stayed in another five minutes and was very agitated, moving around, whimpering more. Finally, he too came out and was also helped by the group.

The twins lay there, side by side, held by a bunch of men.

I asked the second twin to focus and tell us what he had been experiencing when he was by himself in the womb.

He said one word—"abandonment," and broke out crying. His twin held and embraced him, and we all cried. "I'm sorry. I didn't mean to leave you. I still loved you and I always have." The older twin said all this to the younger. They held each other, and there wasn't a dry eye in the circle. We all sang to them:

> Like a ship in the harbor,
> Like a father and child,
> Like a light in the darkness,
> I'll hold you awhile.
> We'll rock on the water,
> I'll cradle you deep

And hold you while angels
Sing you to sleep.

A beatific smile came over the face of the younger twin as the older stroked his beard, mustache, and thinning blonde hair. It was an unforgettable scene.

It made no difference to me whether this re-enactment had any objective reality to it. Who cares? It was a very therapeutic experience for all concerned.

Here is one more example from another healing circle. (The healing circles often lead into expressive work. Kurtz calls it, nicely, "riding the rapids").

She has identified herself as a survivor of childhood sexual abuse although she has no clear memories of the event—just a feeling. She lays down and immediately identifies my assistant (Louis Mezei) as looking like her father. "I can't get his face out of my bed," she says.

I have Louis lay so that just his face is on the mat facing her. There is no time (or need) to ask her how she feels. She begins to cry, scream, moan, shriek, and kick. Another assistant, Selig Broitman, puts a kick bag at her feet and she kicks away.

Then, she stops, and I can see she is feeling something that is difficult to say. I lean over very close to her, remind her where we really are; "We're at Spring Hill and this is a healing circle, and no one is going to really hurt you. Tell me what is happening for you."

She confides in me, "There is a burning pain in my vagina." I nod my head, yes. I ask her if it would be Ok if I had Louis try to pull her legs apart while she tried to keep them together. I tell her that if she does it, she can, at any time, say "STOP, I MEAN IT" and Louis will immediately stop. She will have control. Louis hears my instructions and nods his head. I have a lot of faith in him and would not do this with just anybody assisting me. She rolls her eyes and nods her head yes. (I got this idea from Al Pesso's paper on Abuse (1988), although when I re-read it, I saw that I had gotten it wrong!).

I had Louis start pulling her legs apart. I can't describe the sounds that came out of her. The whole room is filled with them. Louis plays his part to perfection. He accommodates exactly the role she needs. I am the director. After a very short while she motions for him to stop and rolls up into a fetal ball and cries some more. The whole group—mostly women—stays close to her, very caringly and unobtrusively. The bell is about to ring. I'm not sure what reality she is inhabiting so I ask her to tell me her social security number (This is a trick I learned fifteen years before from Armand DiMele as a way to bring a person back to "present time.") She starts to laugh, recites her number, we de-role Louis, and I have never seen her looking so present. I ask if she would like a song. She would and tells me the one she wants. She wants it to be like her husband is singing it to her. We sing to her:

How could anyone ever tell you, that you're anything less than beautiful?
How could anyone ever tell you, that you're less than whole?
How could anyone fail to notice that your loving is a miracle,
How deeply you're connected to my soul.

We hum the verse to her four times, and she seems almost to doze off. Louis and I exchange a nod of mutual respect and collaboration.

This one comes from my private practice:

He is in the midst of deciding to finally separate from his wife after several months of ambivalence. He is carrying a lot of rage. I invite him to place his wife's face on the pillow in front of him and take the bataka. I tell him to close his eyes and remember the last seven months of their marriage. "Just let the memories cross the screen of your awareness, one by one, whatever ones want to walk through." I notice that a few tears drop, and his hands enfold the bataka handle more forcefully. "When you feel ready, open your eyes, see Amanda's face on the pillow and let your body do whatever it wants to do." Soon he is beating up the pillow with gusto as I cheer him on. Days, weeks, months, years of anger, rage, and frustration come pouring out. After awhile he stops beating the pillow and collapses into long-suppressed tears.

When he has had enough time with the tears by himself, I move toward him gently and slowly and cuddle him. He puts his head in my lap and cries even more.

When the tears subside, I ask him to focus. We are both surprised by what he sees. "I see the 1954 All-star Baseball game. My father and I are at it together. Gil McDougal has just made this wicked wonderful play at second base." He is smiling. "Where did that come from?" "Beats me—what is the feeling?" "Like, peaceful. (tears) Like I need to spend time with him and other men (more tears). Like I need to go to a baseball game." "Tomorrow is Opening Day." "Maybe I'll go to Fenway, play hooky from work…My wife never liked baseball."

By this time he is grinning from ear to ear, and it is time for the session to end.

Notice in these sessions how much and what variety of previously blocked emotion is released! I don't want you to think every such session is like this. It isn't. This is hard stuff to get people to do and can be very challenging even to a person as experienced in this work as I am (fifteen years of it).

But when it happens, there is little doubt that something very powerful has happened.

One more example from my private practice. This one allows me to at least allude to my work with focusing, expressive work, and couples.

In my practice these days about three out of fifteen sessions a week are with couples. I have a particular way I begin a first session with couples. After listening to each person talk for awhile about what has brought them to me, I ask them each to close their eyes, imagine their attention is like a searchlight, and first, just see how they each are inside. (This is the first step, of course, of focusing.) After they have done this, I ask for a nod of the head when they are ready to move on.

I wait until they are both ready. Then, I ask them to hold their relationship in front of them, picture it, say their partner's name over and over—whatever will hold it in front of them—and then I say, "And let your attention come down into your body and see what is the whole feel of the relationship for you…(*invitation to focus*) Let a word, phrase, image, sound, or gesture form that will match or act as a handle on the feeling inside…when you get a handle, say it back to yourself, check it against your body, see if it fits….Take your time…you don't have to do it as quickly or slowly as your partner. Give me a nod when you are finished."

When they have each nodded, I may ask one or two further focusing questions—"Ask the feeling—what's the crux of it? What makes it this way?" "Ask it—what does it need? What does it need to have happen?" Or I may simply say, "Now, I want you to open your eyes, turn your chairs to face each other, and take turns—like sharer and witness—telling each other what you have just experienced."

This lesbian couple has come in because one member wants a child and the other does not. They have done the focusing and now are ready—more or less—to talk:

T: Decide who wants to talk first. Talk directly to your partner—unless you want for some reason, at some point, to talk to me. Then, turn your chair so it is facing me. You two decide who goes first.

C1:   (the one who wants a child) I saw us holding a baby
        girl…(tears) and the feeling was in the song lyric, "We Are
        Family." It was warm (more tears) warm in a way my family
        never was.

C2:   (she looks flabbergasted) I saw us holding a baby girl, too. (C1
        now looks shocked) And we were playing with her, and sud-
        denly she wanted to go into your arms, and I felt left out—just
        like I always did growing up. I also heard the lyric, "We Are
        Family" in my head, and I saw—who was it—The Staple
        Singers singing it—(none of us can remember who sings it!) But
        they all had their tongues sticking out at me (cries).

There is an embarrassment of riches here. Remember: It is just a first
session. I decide to go for gestalt expressive work. That is, I focus, and
see inside how to set up a gestalt expressive experiment.

T: Ok. Let's bring that doll over from the corner of the room. I'm
        the doctor so I'll go get it (laughter).

(I bring the doll over) Now I want you to each hold it and talk to it as
if it were the baby you may or may not have.

C1:   (tears throughout) I love you, my darling. You are the little girl
        I always wanted to be. I'll take good care of you. I'll never for-
        get you. I'll never forsake you. We are all going to be family.
        (Gives the doll to C2)

C2:   (can hardly hold her) You are going to come between us. If we
        have you, I'll be the outsider—the father who stays down in the
        cellar watching TV. You'll prefer her to me…and you know
        what? (This comes like a revelation to her)…I won't like you so
        much either. (She hands the doll to me.)

T: (to doll) Well, I guess we see where we stand at this point (C1
        and C2 nod their heads in agreement). But don't worry.
        Remember: this isn't about you; it's about them. Now, this is

just where we will all start. Let's keep an open mind—and open hearts—as to where we will end up.

I saw them for seven months, once a week. They never missed a session. This was in 1998.

Last month I got a postcard with a baby shower announcement from them.

Table 3 summarizes the characteristics of expressive work, its results, and a sampling of kinds of expressive work I make frequent use of, and where each comes from.

Table 3—Expressive Technique

Characteristics:	symbolic action
	use of arms and legs and other body parts
Results:	finishing unfinished business
	going beyond point of self-interruption
Examples:	*Gestalt:* repetition; amplification; exaggeration; presentification; "let me feed you a sentence…"; "speak directly to_____.
	Psychodrama: role-playing; re-creation of crucial scenes
	Bioenergetics: "abandonment" stress position (this is expressive and hard)
	Pesso: accommodation

◆

I hope the last three sections have given you a feel for what body-centered focusing-oriented therapy is like as I have practiced it. It is some of the best work I have done. As I age and my body feels more fragile, I do less of it. Alas.

Please remember that these examples are illustrative, not exhaustive, and, obviously, I have chosen to share ones I feel particularly good about.

Not all the sessions are like these. I make mistakes. Things don't work. I can't get a handle on what is happening. People refuse to follow my invitations. People aren't sufficiently warmed up. There is reluctance. People just won't let themselves do it.

This kind of therapy is not an unending string of successful, dramatic, and stirring interactions. It is work. At times it is hard work. It continues to be some of the best work I know.

Conclusion

Let me summarize what I have said thus far:

There exists in the world a brand new perspective on therapy. It is called Focusing-Oriented Therapy (FOT).

It can also be called Felt Sense-Oriented Therapy. It comes out of Dr. Eugene Gendlin's discovery of the felt sense, focusing, and the experiential method.

The therapeutic relationship is central to FOT.

Focusing and listening are the main methods in FOT.

Focusing-Oriented Therapy is friendly to the integration of many different methods, and in fact invites other practitioners to combine methods they already know with focusing and listening.

Whether these are verbal or body-centered methods they are welcome.

Focusing-Oriented Therapy is an attempt to bring client and therapist in tune for at least parts of every session with the ongoing bodily-felt experiencing process that goes on in each of us. Focusing-Oriented Therapy helps carry that experiencing process forward so that the client can have the experience of real change happening.

I want to add one more thing about how I do therapy.

One of my hard, hardy, and hearty long-term client's suggested I include some examples of the lengths I will go to for clients.

For this client who at the age of fifty-three was just considering moving out of his parents' home but did not know how to go about finding his own place, I drove thirty miles to where he lived and spent one Saturday afternoon showing him how to find an apartment and going with him to look at a few. I thought of this as helping him jump-start his ratty old car.

With a very alone client whose birthday was very near my own, we had a joint birthday celebration every year for awhile, going to a club, having dinner together, going to a movie. We both enjoyed these events. I should add that after each of the extra-curricular events I am telling you about, in the very next therapy session, I always explored how the event impacted on the therapy.

With a folklorist who sang with an East African band once a month in my neighborhood, I went once at her invitation to see the performance, mingle with the performers, and meet her friends.

With a former client who had made a serious suicide attempt, I visited him while he was still strapped to a gurney with a police guard. I listened to his story of a harrowing two day multi-modal suicide effort. The only thing I said was that there was one way that he could have done the job for sure—by burning down his house with him in it—and, since he did not do that obvious thing, there must have been one part of him at least that wanted to live. When he recovered from his injuries and came back to see me for therapy, he told me my visit and the one thing I said had started him back on the road to recovery. He now leads a productive and successful life with some pleasure and happiness.

With two clients I visited their houses to see for myself just what they were telling me about the clutter and how difficult it was to get rid of it. After I saw their houses I understood their dilemma much better.

When I have birthday parties I invite selected clients who I think can handle the situation and mingle with other people in my life. Again, I check in with them after to see what effect this has had on the therapy. This way, even if I have made a mistake, I get to apologize for it and we look and see what can be done if anything needs to be done to reconstruct our therapeutic alliance. I have only had one time when there was recuperative work to be done. The overall response has been gratitude that I am willing to open my life up to them as I am.

I am highlighting here what I might call 'unconventional' or dual relationships with clients (Lazarus and Zur 2002). One can have impeccable boundaries and selective dual relationships. Not exploiting the client is key. Please remember that Freud took some of his favorite clients on vacation with his family.

I remember my college advisor, Dick Jones, talking about a very difficult case that he considered a failure despite lots of good work that had gone into it. The client always wanted Dick to go for a walk with him outside while they did therapy. Dick interpreted this wish over and over again. The fellow never dropped it. Dick said that if he had it to do over he would simply have taken a walk with the guy and done therapy on the walk. He had been too bound by tradition to the office.

We can leave our offices and continue to do therapy.

◆

I feel reluctant to end this book. I remember reading that Ernest Hemingway said he had trouble finishing *For Whom The Bell Tolls* because he hesitated to kill off the main character, Robert Jordan, at the end of the book. Hemingway said that he had lived with Jordan for so long and grown so fond of him that he was sad to see him go. It was a loss.

Such is how I feel about ending this book. All endings are little deaths and all beginnings are, as Tennyson said, The new sun rising, bringing a new day.

Wednesday March 29, 2006

Appendices

Appendix A:
A Roadmap to Gendlin's Focusing-Oriented Psychotherapy

Since 1997 Joan Klagsbrun and I have run trainings on Focusing-Oriented Therapy (FOT). From this has gradually emerged a "roadmap" to the book, *Focusing-Oriented Psychotherapy*, which is, of course, our main text.

Here is that roadmap for your consideration.

The reason for the roadmap is that Gene's book is brilliant. dense, and difficult. Anything that helps with understanding it is useful. I hope this will do that.

The place to start the book is at chapter twenty-three, "The Client-Therapist Relationship". In this chapter Gene says that the relationship of therapist and client comes first. "Interpersonal interaction is the most important therapeutic avenue" (p.283). In this chapter Gene talks about the worst kind of therapeutic relationship (one that mimics a teacherish parent-child relationship) and the ingredients of a good therapeutic relationship, one that touches "the person in there".

Understanding this chapter is central to getting the whole of the book.

After, comes Part One on focusing and listening. Focusing and listening are the main methods of Gendlin's FOT. He says in chapter twenty three that "In therapy the relationship (the person in there) is of first importance, listening comes second, and focusing instructions come only third" (p.297).

The name "felt-sense-oriented therapy" is cumbersome but what it has going for it is that Gendlin does put the felt sense as the primary term for the way he would combine and integrate all kinds of therapy. He says that different kinds of therapy "can consist of totally different kinds of experience. I call these therapeutic 'avenues'. If we think of ourselves as working with the client's felt sense, then each avenue becomes a way to lead to a felt sense. And, once there is a felt sense, all avenues are means of carrying the felt sense forward" (170-171).

The first chapter of Part Two is the linchpin from focusing and listening to other psychotherapeutic methods. Gendlin talks about procedures and avenues of therapy. "Therapy can consist of totally different kinds of experience. I call these therapeutic 'avenues'. A given therapeutic event can consist of feelings, emotions, images, role play, words, cognitive beliefs, memories, catharsis, interpersonal interactions, dreams, dance moves, muscle movement, and habitual behavior." The link is the felt sense. It is the target, the aim of different therapeutic interventions. Gendlin says that FOT can also learn from each of the other methods. He also says that FOT is not the only way to do therapy helpfully.

I think this sentence is quite important: "No one has the right to claim that there is only one way for human beings to grow, in therapy, or in personal development, or in anything" (108).

There follow six chapters (12-17) on other avenues of therapy, which can be utilized in a felt sense-oriented way.

Then comes what I think should be Part Three of the book. That is, I don't think it is just a two-part book. I think part three is chapters 19-23.

The chapters on the critic and the life-forward direction are the main ones there for me. These are aspects of Gendlin's FOT that I don't have a good name for. I will call them, tentatively, special aspects of Gendlin's FOT.

Gendlin's chapter on the critic can be usefully compared with Ann Weiser Cornell's approach in The Radical Acceptance of Everything (See, "Radical Gentleness…").

In chapter twenty-four, the last chapter, Gendlin argues that not all that happens in therapy is therapeutic. He wants the therapist to get past 'the formal dance' that is an obstacle to real relating. He is not arguing that therapy is the same as friendship, but he is pointing to some of the negative aspects that go along with being labeled 'a therapist doing 'therapy'.

I hope this summary helps you in following Gendlin's text. The book, I think, is brilliant. Perhaps the roadmap will help readers traverse the rocky and perilous terrain that the book seeks to cover.

Appendix: B
Focusing Instructions

(There is nothing sacred about any particular focusing instructions. These are simply what I like and use now.)

1. Saying hello: *Find a comfortable position...Relax and close your eyes...Take a few deep breaths...Let your attention follow the breath down into your body...and when you're ready just ask, "How am I inside right now?" Don't answer. Give an answer time to form in your body...imagine your attention is like a searchlight and you can turn it on and shine it into your inside feeling place and just greet whatever you find there...Practice taking a friendly attitude toward whatever is there...(30 seconds of silence)*

2. Clearing a space...Making a list (optional): *Now, imagine yourself sitting on a park bench. Ask yourself, "What's in the way between me and feeling all fine right now?" Let whatever comes up, come up. Don't go inside any particular thing right now. Just stack each thing at a comfortable distance from you on the bench...Take inventory: "What's between me and feeling all fine right now?" [or "What are the main things..."] If the list stops, ask, "Except for that am I all fine?" If more comes up, add it to the stack. Stay distanced from your stack. Give me a signal when you're ready for the next step.*

3. Picking A problem: *Now, feel yourself as if magnetically pulled toward the one thing in the stack that most needs your attention right now...If you have any trouble letting it choose you, ask, "What is worst?" (or, "What is best?"—good feelings can be worked with too!)..."What most needs some work right now?"..."What won't let go of me?"...Pick one thing. (pause). Let me know when you have one....*

4. Letting the felt sense form: *Now ask, "What does this whole thing feel like?"..."What is the whole feel of it?" Don't answer with what you* *already know about it. Listen to your body…Sense the issue freshly…Give your body thirty seconds to a minute for the feel of "all of that" to form.*

5. Finding the handle: *Find a word, phrase, image, sound or gesture that feels like it matches, comes from, or will act as a handle on the felt sense, the whole feel of it. Keep your attention on the area in your body where you feel it, and just let a word, phrase, image, sound or gesture appear that feels like a good match for the feeling sense inside.*

6. Resonating the handle: *Now, say the word, phrase, image, sound or gesture back to yourself…Check it against your body…See if there is a sense of "rightness of fit",…an inner "yes, that's it"…If there isn't, gently let go of that handle and let one that fits better appear.*

7. Asking and receiving: *Now we are going to ask the felt sense some questions. Some it will answer. Some it won't. Don't be concerned about questions it does not answer. Receive whatever answers it gives. Ask the questions with an expectantly friendly attitude and be receptive to whatever it sends you.*

Ask, "What's the crux of this feeling?" "What's the main thing about it?" Don't answer with your head; let the body feeling answer.

And ask, "What's the worst of this feeling?" "What makes it so bad?" Wait…

And ask, "What's wrong?" Imagine the felt sense as a shy child sitting on a stoop. It needs caring encouragement to speak. Go over to it, sit down, and gently ask, "What's wrong?" Wait…

And ask, "What does this feeling need?"

And now ask, "What is a good small step in the right direction for this thing?" "What is a small (emphasis) step in the direction of fresh air?"

Ask, "What needs to happen?" "What actions need to be taken?"

And now ask, "What would my body feel like if this thing were all better, all resolved?" Move your body into the position or posture it would be in if this thing were all cleared up. This is called looking the answer up in the back of the book. Now, from this position, ask, "What's between me and here?" "What's in the way of it being all Ok?" Wait…

Finally, ask your felt sense space to send you the exactly right focusing question you need at this moment. If it does, ask the felt sense that question.

Don't answer with your head. Just hang out with the felt sense, keep it company, let it respond. Wait...

8. Coming back: *Ok, now you have a minute to use however you'd like. Some people find it useful to retrace the steps they've come. Some like to stretch and relax. Some find it useful to underline the furthest place they've come to; pitch a tent there so you can come back to it if you want...Use this minute however you would like and then open your eyes...and this round of focusing is over.*

Notes

Introduction

1.   Another formulation of the nature of FOT would be:

Focusing-Oriented therapy is a therapy whose basic approach comes from Eugene Gendlin's book Focusing-Oriented Psychotherapy. In this therapy, the therapist-client relationship is of primary importance, and the basic methods used are focusing and listening. Beyond that, focusing-oriented therapies can look quite different from each other depending upon what other methods are combined with the basic FOT methods. However, the attempt to give "an experiential response" ought to bring a base-line commonality to the therapist's actions in any sub-type of Focusing-Oriented Therapy.

Gendlin as Therapist

1.   I do not want to go too deeply into Gendlin's philosophical writings. It is important to say that his basic concepts are *interactional*. Marion Hendricks writes that "It is a powerful philosophical move to put activity or interaction as the basic, first term. It gives us concepts modeled on humans, rather than on mathematical units. The unit model of our atomistic science has great power in relation to machines, but it is inadequate to understand people." A 'first-person' science requires a different kind of basic concept than does a mechanistic science. See Marion Hendricks, "Research Basis of Focusing-Oriented Experiential Psychology"(2002).

Focusing

1.   In this and all other clinical examples changes have been made to protect the identity of the client.

2.   I do not want to oversell focusing. Let me add two caveats about relying on it too much.

Focusing can have an autistic quality to it and so is probably not the method of choice by itself with autistic or Asperger syndrome people. By 'an autistic quality' to it, I am referring to the person's eyes being closed and going only into inner space and trying to block out outer space, including the therapist. Autistic people do this naturally and eventually relating them to the world outside ought to be an aim.

Similarly, some people have to talk in therapy. That is what they come for. For example, one client is in a life-situation about which he feels he has no one with whom he can safely share. In therapy he can share it. That is what he needs from me. I may now and then introduce a focusing step in order to help him go deeper. But, more often than not he simply wants a sympathetic, empathetic and non-judgmental ear to listen to his unusual and quite compelling story.

Listening

1.   On Rogers as listener cf.: "Rogers was a great listener. This was one of my first impressions of him. I had driven across the country to visit him and [his wife] Helen…When I arrived, Helen was occupied with a friend, so Rogers and I went into his study to talk for about forty-five minutes. When he came out to join Helen, he summarized our conversation for her by reviewing all the major points I had made during those forty-five minutes. I remember my astonishment, thinking, 'My God, this man *really* heard everything I said! What an incredible listener he is!' Then I laughed at myself for reacting this way, remembering why I had traveled across the country to meet him."

"Norman Rice…remembered…'I came to Carl and asked him if he might be able to work me into one or more counseling interviews, since I had never experienced him directly as a therapist. He managed to work in four. At the end of the first session with Carl, I came out to Virginia Hallman, his secretary, and practically shouted, "Now I know the secret ingredient!" She was kind of low-key and gave me a "What's with you?" response. I told her I have never felt so deeply and fully understood and so completely respected in all my life, and that the effect on me was electrifying" (Kirschenbaum 1979, 178).

And: "What is obvious about Rogers, in the Gloria films for example, is that he listens: he really tries to understand Gloria and accept her without conditions. What is most obvious in Rogers is *the self-transcendent quality of his empathetic attitude*. It almost seems that he disappears. He himself has said that it is difficult for him to describe afterwards what happened in a therapy session" (in Levant and Shlein 1984, 219, emphasis mine).

2.   From a slightly different angle, Cf. Mathieu-Coughlin and Klein:

"The history of the experiencing construct forms an interesting lattice between the work of Rogers and Gendlin."

"…Rogers defined pathology as 'incongruence' between awareness and experience, but he lacked a way to define the term 'experience' in observable terms, so that 'congruence' with it could be measured. The hidden storehouse could not be observed and compared with aware experience. This problem was solved by Gendlin's definition of implicitly complex experiencing…as the basic felt datum or referent of awareness"(in Rice and Greenberg eds. 1984, 214-215).

3.   Listening is a very subtle art. On paper it can look deceptively easy and resistible. Invariably, when I teach listening someone says, "I

don't want to just say back a person's words. Anyone can do that. And what good would that do anyway?"

Two points: try out both listening and being listened to.

Doing it well is much harder than the simplistic (and inaccurate) description "say it back" indicates.

And the experience of being listened to is most important. One must experience how it feels to be on the receiving end of listening. I continue to be surprised at how special it feels and how useful it is when I get well listened to.

4.   With regard to selectivity in listening (or, when to paraphrase) remember: "We are experience [Gendlin would say 'experiencing'] oriented. Not every statement of the client receives equal attention. We always try to shift from the narrative to the feelings, from the theoretical-abstract level to what is concretely lived through" (Lietaer, in Levant and Shlein eds. 1984, 51).

5.   My writings on The Heart Workshop, YOU CANNOT STAY ON THE SUMMIT FOREVER (1987) and A REMEMBRANCE: SPRING HILL AND OPENING THE HEART (1998) are available from me.

The Integration of Focusing and Listening and Other Verbal Interventions

1.   This sentence is clearly presumptuous. I mean that the chances of my being wrong at these times feels like no more than 1%.

2.   I might have said "and your feelings get lost?" with the question mark, tentatively, as it does seem to be an interpretation (that proves to be right on target). The important thing though is that the client accepts the interpretation and it carries forward her experiencing.

3.   I could have reflected, "Oh, so you are in *a whole new place…*"
The rule here would be: Always reflect forward movement; don't be
too pain-centered.

4.   A good example of "listening for the implicit." The "uncomfortable" is the therapist's reading into the client's words. The therapist
needs to check carefully that the client is *really* accepting the therapist's
explications rather than merely agreeing so as to be polite.

5.   Alternatively: "So *retelling* helps get you in touch…what's there
now?" This would be an example of a reflection followed by an invitation to focus, an invitation that seems to follow well in the direction of
the reflection.

6.   The preceding interactions illustrate focusing followed by listening. Staying with this image I could have in a gestalt way invited her
to be the old dried up lemon and see what she experiences as it. Instead,
I notice that the client is holding her throat as she is talking at this point
and this awareness guides my next intervention. Notice how the therapist is aware of the client's body movements and makes use of them.

7.   Notice that after a gestalt action segment, T invites C to focus. That
is one pattern in how focusing and listening and gestalt go together.

8.   I might have reflected here just what the C says: "You're mourning…there's a sadness and a question 'Can I accept that this is the way
it is?'" It is not clear to me whether my interpretation here is correct.
The client may be thrown off by it but then returns to her own track.

9.   Some new insights ("I see now…") have come to C as a by-
product of deeply experiencing the feelings which at the start of the
session ("everything is external") she was far away from.

10.   Joan Klagsbrun initiated my annual visit to her Focusing class at Lesley College—kind of "meet the author and watch him work" night. Thanks, Joan, for the opportunity. This particular year Joan was on sabbatical and Kathy taught the class and kept the annual visit going.

11.   I want to say that I think my listening responses were especially sharp and poetic in this session and that really helped carry it as far as it went.

The Integration of Focusing and Listening and Other Body-Centered Therapeutic Interventions

1.   This entire section follows closely the article, "Focusing and Bodywork," which I wrote with Laury Rappaport for the Focusing Connection (vol. III, No. 2, May 1985). I want to acknowledge and thank Laury for her collaboration with me on this article. It was very much a mutual piece of work.

2.   I want to add at length about what Focusing and Hakomi have to offer each other:
Of all the body-oriented therapies, Hakomi is the most congruent with Focusing. Hakomi and Focusing meet in their core principles.

Both therapies are very respectful of and supportive to the specific client. They are tailor-made rather than off-the-rack therapies. They are both non-violent and utilize some eyes-closed processes to help the person into a state of consciousness in which inner data can be accessed and processed.

What does Focusing have to offer Hakomi: Kurtz calls Hakomi "assisted meditation." That is, the therapist does something (e.g. says a probe) which the client is then invited to process in a meditative state. This is not totally unlike Pesso or the bioenergetic therapist "doing" something to which the client responds.

But, the Focusing therapist does something less than the Hakomi therapist. He is less active in the creation of experience. His activity is more restricted to asking focusing questions and receiving and reflecting clients' responses. The Hakomi therapist has more input in the form of a probe or a "little experiment." The Focusing therapist does less evoking than does the Hakomi therapist. He asks: "What is there?" (Of course, the very asking can be seen as evocative but less so than a Hakomi probe.)

And what does Hakomi have to offer when it is combined with Focusing? Focusing therapy can tend to be too passive, too reactive. The pure Focusing therapist has to wait till the client brings up X upon which to focus. The Focusing therapist waits and reflects, but what if the client does not bring up, say, his tendency to miss appointments or her cocaine habit or wonderings about incest? The pure Focusing therapist wants to be in the position to ask, "What is the whole feel of X?" but tends to be constrained by whether or not the client brings up X. The Hakomi therapist is not so constrained. He can choose to use a probe to evoke an experience about which there are behavioral cues or about which he simply has a hunch; e.g., "What happens for you when I say...it is Ok to have needs," even though the person has never directly said, "I can't have any needs." The Hakomi therapist can "go fishing"; he has latitude to be more expansive and creative than the strictly Focusing therapist would be...and the Focusing therapist reminds him how dangerous over-use of such latitude can be.

3.   I want to digress for a moment about the suspicion many therapists (and clients) have about body-centered therapy. Of course, the most basic reason for this suspicion is that sex is of the body, and therefore, to bring the body into treatment means to have to confront sex. It is absolutely crucial that there be no erotic element in the touching at all. Yet, there is another reason, historically, for the wariness of many therapists to body-oriented therapy. Wilhelm Reich is really the historical personage most identified with body-oriented therapy. That does

not give it a great pedigree. Reich finished out his life in prison, and, while he worked, as a sympathetic biographer has written, "In therapy, as in most of his other endeavors, Reich was a man of extremes. At his best, he played in a league all his own. At his worst, he made mistakes a first-year psychiatric resident...wouldn't make" (Sharaf, p. 243).

I think that this reputation for inconsistency has fallen over body-centered therapies as a whole and contributes to the distrust of them. I think some of this distrust is merited. The abuse of body-oriented therapies can be even more harmful than abuse of verbal therapy—although that abuse can be plenty bad, too! And the training of body-oriented therapists has not tended to be as rigorous or professional as that of verbal therapists. But this is changing, and training is not everything! (For more on the ethics of body-oriented therapy, see Smith 1985, chapter 10).

4.   Notice how focusing often fits at the start and the end of hard and expressive sessions. This is when the sessions go easily and really flow. Many don't. The examples I've quoted are among my all-time favorites—times when we "rode the rapids" with little obstruction. When there is more obstruction, more reluctance, more resistance, more unclarity—then there is more focusing and listening off and on during the session—whenever they are needed to help us get back on track.

5.   Kathy McGuire has similar things to say re Gendlin and emotion in her valuable chapter, "Affect in Focusing and Experiential Psychotherapy" (in Safran and Greenberg 1991).
She had Gendlin read and comment upon a draft of her chapter and then write his own free-standing chapter ("On Emotion in Psychotherapy").

She writes, "Gendlin...does not give value to the changing, healing quality of the tears, sobbing, and laughter.... He equates this kind of catharsis with the non-productive repeating of the emotion.... This author would like him to give more attention to the qualitatively different nature of these two forms of emotion" (p. 233).

"Gendlin emphases the slow steps of direct reference and not dramatic moments of catharsis…." (p. 236).

And Gendlin writes back to her:

"If you want it to be me, do not move from emotion to felt sense. The hardest way to get a felt sense is from emotion—one has to pull the whole thing out first, usually, *pull out of the emotion* (ital. in the original), then get a felt sense directly, or from an image of the whole thing" (p. 248).

McGuire writes that her dialogue with Gendlin indicates to her, "the need for the creation of a new conceptual category, one that distinguishes between emotion that repeats in an unchanging fashion and emotion that is part of a healing change process" (p. 248).

She goes on to say that Gendlin is really most interested in what she calls quite nicely "a…nonemotional felt event,"—the felt sense. This leads him to undervalue the emotional felt event—catharsis.

The dialogue (of sorts) between McGuire and Gendlin is fascinating although not always clear, and, to use a phrase impishly, "well-focused." It is well-worth reading as a starting place to see where the important issues of focusing, emotion, catharsis, and psychotherapy stand within the focusing-oriented therapy community as of 1999.

A further source of difficulty: Gendlin says that "at times" the felt sense might "best be described in words that are also the names of emotions, for example scared, shameful, or guilty. Even so," he continues, "it contains a whole intricacy of elements, not only what the emotion of the same name would contain." (Focusing-Oriented Psychotherapy, p. 59) This is very important. To me it means that "emotion names" can be the names both of emotions and felt senses. In other words the culprit, so to speak, is not the emotion name itself but *how it is dealt with by the therapist and client.* If they treat it like a felt sense, i.e., look for the 'moreness' of it, then the emotion name is itself considered a felt sense and the previously black vs. white discrimination of emotion from felt sense becomes more gray.

References

Angyal, Andras. NEUROSIS AND TREATMENT. New York: Wiley, 1965.

Bean, O. ME AND THE ORGONE. New York: St. Martin's Press, 1978.

Bergin, A. and Garfield, S.(Eds.) HANDBOOK OF PSYCHOTHERAPY AND BEHAVIOR CHANGE. New York: John Wiley, 1971.

Bozarth, J. D. "Beyond Reflection: Emergent Modes of Empathy." In R. Levant and J. M. Shlein (Eds.) CLIENT-CENTERED THERAPY AND THE PERSON-CENTERED APPROACH. New York: Praeger, 1984.

Cain, D. J. & Seeman, J. (Eds.) HUMANISTIC PSYCHOTHERAPIES; Handbook of Research and Practice. Washington, D.C. APA, 2001.

Cornell, Ann Weiser. THE FOCUSING STUDENT'S MANUAL PART TWO: LISTENING. Berkeley 1993.

Cornell, Ann Weiser. THE POWER OF FOCUSING. California: New Harbinger Press, 1995.

Cornell, Ann Weiser. THE RADICAL ACCEPTANCE OF EVERY-THING. Berkeley, California: Calluna Press, 2005.

Eysenck, H.J. The Effects of Psychotherapy. In Eysenck, J.H. HANDBOOK OF ABNORMAL PSYCHOLOGY. New York: Basic Books, 1961.

Frank, J.D. PERSUASION AND HEALING; A COMPARATIVE STUDY OF PSYCHOTHERAPY. Baltimore, John Hopkins University Press, 1973.

Friedman, N. "The Genius of Andras Angyal" written in 1975 published in THERAPEUTIC ESSAYS. New York: Half-Court Press, 1981.

Friedman, N. "Harold and Maude: My Experiential Therapy with Leida Berg". Review of Existential Psychology and Psychiatry. Vol. XVII, Nos.2 & 3. 1980-1981.

Friedman, N. OPENING THE HEART. Ashby, Ma.: Spring Hill Press (pamphlet) 1981.

Friedman, N. EXPERIENTIAL THERAPY AND FOCUSING. New York: Half Court Press, 1982.

Friedman, N. "On Focusing." Journal of Humanistic Psychology, Vol. 26, No. 2, Winter, 1986, pp. 103-111.

Friedman, N. FOCUSING: SELECTED ESSAYS 1974-1999. Philadelphia: Xlibris, 2000.

Friedman, N. and Rapapport, Laury, "Focusing and Bodywork". The Focusing Connection, May, 1985, Vol. III, No. 2 pp.1-3.

Gendlin, E.T. "Experiencing: A Variable in the Process of Therapeutic Change," American Journal of Psychotherapy, Vol. XV, No. 2, April 1, 1961.

Gendlin, E.T. "Psychotherapeutic Experiences with Schizophrenics" in Rogers, Carl (Ed.) THE THERPAEUTIC RELATIOINSHIP AND ITS IMPACT: A STUDY OF PSYCHOTHERAPY WITH SCHIZOPHRENICS. Madison, Wisconsin: University of Wisconsin Press, 1967.

Gendlin, E.T., "The Experiential Response." In Hammer, (Ed.) THE USE OF INTERPRETATION IN TREATMENT. New York, Grune and Stratton Inc., 1968.

Gendlin, E.T., "Experiential Psychotherapy" in Corsini, CURRENT PSY-CHOTHERAPIES. Itasca, Illinois: F.E. Peacock. 1974, pp. 317-32.

Gendlin, E.T. FOCUSING. New York: Bantam Books, 1981.

Gendlin, E.T. "On Emotion in Therapy." In Safran and Greenberg (eds.), EMOTION, PSYCHOTHERAPY, and CHANGE. New York: The Guilford Press. 1991, pp. 255-279.

Gendlin E.T. FOCUSING-ORIENTED PYCHOTHERAPY. New York: Guilford, 1996.

Gendlin, E.T. EXPERIENCING AND THE CREATION OF MEANING. Evanston, Illinois: Northwestern University Press, 1997 (Originally published by The Free Press, 1961).

Gurban,A.& Razin,A.(Eds.) EFFECTIVE PSYCHOTHERAPY London: Pergamon Press, 1977.

Hart, J. "The Development of Client-Centered Therapy" in J. Hart and T. Tomlinson. NEW DEVELOPMENTS IN CLIENT_CENTERED THERAPY. Boston: Houghton-Mifflin, 1970.

Hendricks, Marion. "Research Basis of Focusing-Oriented Experiential Psychotherapy." In HUMANISTIC PSYCHOTHERAPIES: HANDBOOK OF RESEARCH AND PRACTICE, David J. Cain (Ed.), Julius Seeman (Assoc. Ed.) PCCS Books, 2002, pp.221-251.

Holmes, J THE SEARCH FOR THE SECURE BASE: ATTACHMENT THEORY AND PSYCHOTHERAPY. East Sussex: Brunner-Rutledge, 2000.

Hubble, M., Duncan, L., Miller, S. (Eds.) THE HEART AND SOUL OF CHANGE: WHAT WORKS IN THERAPY. Washington, D.C. APA, 1999.

Kempler, W. EXPERIENTIAL PSYCHOTHERAPY WITH FAMILIES. New York: Brunner/Mazel, 1981.

Kirschenbaum, H. ON BECOMING CARL ROGERS New York: Delacorte Press. 1997.

Kurtz, R. BODY-CENTERED PSYCHOTHERAPY; THE HAKOMI METHOD. Mendocino: Life Rhythm, 1991.

Lazarus, A. and Zur, O. (Eds.) DUAL RELATIONSHIPS AND PSY-CHOTHERAPY. New York: Springer, 2002.

Levant, R. & Shlein, J. M. (Eds.) CLIENT-CENTERED THERAPY AND THE PERSON-CENTERED APPROACH. New York: Praeger. 1984.

Mahrer, A.R. EXPERIENCING. New York: Brunner-Mazel, 1978.

McGuire, K. (1974) Listening and Being Listened To. Building Supportive Community. Cambridge: Supportive Community Project, 1981.

McKenna, P.A. and Todd, D.M. Longitudinal utilization of mental health services: a time-line method, nine retrospective accounts, and a preliminary conceptualization. Psychotherapy Research, 7,pp. 383-396.

Miller, S., Duncan, B. & Hubble, M. ESCAPE FROM BABEL New York: Norton, 1997.

Naranjo, C. THE TECHNIQUES OF GESTALT THERAPY. Berkeley: SAT Press, n.d.

Nathan, P.E.& Gorman, J.M. (Eds.) A GUIDE TO TREATMENTS THAT WORK. New York: Oxford Press, 2002.

Norcross,J.C (Ed.) PSYCHOTHERAPY RELATIONSHIPS THAT WORK. New York, Oxford University Press, 2002.

Pesso, A. Sexual Abuse. Strolling Woods. Franklin, N.H., 1988.

Raskin, N. Studies on Psychotherapeutic Orientation: Ideology in Practice AAP Psychotherapy Research Monographs. Orlando, 1974.

Rilke, R. SELECTED POEMS. London: Penguin, 1994.

Rogers, C. ON BECOMING A PERSON. Boston: Houghton Mifflin, 1961.

Rogers, C. ON PERSONAL POWER. New York: Delacorte Press,1977.

Rogers, C. A WAY OF BEING. Boston: Houghton Mifflin, 1980.

Rogers, C. and Meader, Betty. "Person-Centered Therapy" In R. Corsini (Ed.). CURRENT PSYCHOTHERAPIES. Itasca: F.E. Peacock, 1979.

Rosenzweig, S. "Some Implicit Common Factors in Diverse Methods of Therapy." American Journal of Orthopsychiatry, 6, 412-415, 1936.

Rowan, J. and Jacobs, M. THE THERAPIST'S USE OF SELF. Buckingham, England: Open University Press, 2002.

Schuster, R. "Empathy and Mindfulness." Journal of Humanistic Psychology. 19 (1), 1979.

Shaw, J.J. and Wheelis, Joan (Eds.) ODYSEES IN PSYCHOTHERAPY. New York, Ardent Media Inc, 2000.

Smith, E.W.L. THE BODY IN PSYCHOTHERAPY. North Carolina: McFarlane, 1985.

Smith, E.W.L., Clance, Pauline Rose, and Imes, Suzanne (Eds.) TOUCH IN PSYCHOTHERAPY. New York: Guilford, 1998.

Wile, D. AFTER THE HONEYMOON. New York: John Wiley, 1988.

Acknowledgements

To: Eugene Gendlin whose theorizing, therapy, and training are the source of this presentation. I love you, Gene, with all your oh-so-human foibles and fallibilities. I hope you really like this book and I can take it if you do not. Consider it an 80th birthday present.

Joan Klagsbrun: I have known you for thirty—some years since we met next to Gene's refrigerator in his Waterside apartment. You have been my ally, confidante, bridge to the Focusing Institute and network, source of referrals and trainees, and all in all the person who brought me back to focusing after Spring Hill's time was up. We have had our spats and genuine differences. I value the way we have stuck with each other until we each felt heard and acknowledged. Mere words cannot do justice to my debt to you or my love for you.

Ann Weiser-Cornell: You have published fifteen of my essays in The Focusing Connection, provided the ingenious solution when my hearing aid failed at the conference at Asilomar; and you have given so much to focusing. Bless you.

Mako Hikasa: You did the Japanese translation of Focusing: Selected Essays with such integrity. I love it when I get notes from people over there that say, "You are very famous in Japan", (although I always want to ask whether that will help me get referrals in Arlington!) Mako, you are an international treasure and I hope you will get recognized as such by all.

Lynn Preston: In the 1970s you shared focusings and listenings and trips on the Staten Island ferry. Your support helped this all happen. (And so, of course, I blame you for everything that has gone wrong!)

Eileen Kenney: You were my first focusing partner and I will always remember among other things wonderful Friday lunches at the Buffalo Roadhouse.

Zack Boukydis: You have been a wonderful focusing-listening partner and buddy.

All the trainees from 1998-2006 (and still counting) who made Joan and my trainings such memorable events.

And for Joe Kern and Jill Cannon: You have made presentations at the trainings that I have made use of specifically in this book. Joe, now we have to approach the Brothers of the Weston Priory and teach them focusing. Jill: You are so precious to me, for all these years, such an indomitable spirit and such commitment to your own growth. I very much admire you.

And to Laury Rappaport: I will always remember and treasure our years of focusing and listening and leading Spring Hill and Heart Workshops together.

And to Obi and Beatrice Falaige: Your West Indian-flavored Joe's Coffee House in Somerville served as my writing office for so many years and reminded me why the Caribbean is such a favorite locale of mine.

Roger Gumley: for enthusiastic, timely and only slightly humbling aid with the computer on which I wrote much of this book.

April Walker: for innovative website management. (Now, if only we could figure out how to sell some of those books…)

Massachusetts Psychological Association: for dues abatements when necessary and the umbrella of legal support provided when needed.

Dean Abby: for the start up (I believe) and keep up of the MSPP Continuing Education Program and for your inclusion of focusing in your table of contents each quarter, crisply displayed. Also, for making presenting at MSPP such a delight (and for the fruit, nuts, cookies, and other assorted goodies left out in the kitchen area…)

Susan Krinsky: for showing me another useful way of doing therapy.

Carole and Frank: So that there is on longer the rumor that I am an only child:):) I count you two as blessings in my life.

And Sue and Alex and Gail and Jeremy too.

Kyra, Zoe, and Gemma: You live in my heart.
As do you, Hope.
And you, Kate.

About the Author

Neil Friedman has a Ph.D. in Clinical Psychology from Harvard University (1965). He has taught at Miles College and Tuskegee Institute in Alabama and at the New School for Social Research, Brandeis, SUNY Stony Brook, and Lesley University. Since 1976, Neil has been in the private practice of psychotherapy with individuals and couples. From 1982 through 1997 he was a staff member of the Opening the Heart workshop at Spring Hill conference center, where he was Co-Director from 1985 to 1988. Neil is a certifying coordinator for the Focusing Institute and a Diplomate of the American Psychotherapy Association. Neil is the author of ten books and over fifty articles. Neil loved Miles College and Spring Hill and loves Focusing and Opening the Heart work. Neil can be found on the Internet at www.neilheart.com. where all his books are for sale. His popular relationship column, "Ask Dr. Neil," can be found at www.Relationship-Talk.com Neil has two daughters, Kyra and Zoe, and a granddaughter, Gemma, all of whom are very, very special and dear to him.

The author would like in future editions of this book to fix any errors that exist in this one. Contacting him at **neilheart@verizon.net** with information about errors would be appreciated, as would any other comments you would like to make.

978-0-595-39830-0
0-595-39830-8